Activity Workbook

ExpressWays

Second Edition

1

Steven J. Molinsky
Bill Bliss

Contributing Author
Dorothy Lynde

Longman

Publisher: *Louisa B. Hellegers*
Electronic Production Editor: *Paula D. Williams*
Manufacturing Manager: *Ray Keating*

Electronic Art Production Supervision: *Todd Ware*
Electronic Art Production/Scanning: *Marita Froimson*
Art Director: *Merle Krumper*
Interior Design: *Ken Liao*

Illustrator: *Richard Hill*

The authors gratefully acknowledge the contribution of Tina Carver
in the development of the *ExpressWays* program.

ISBN 0-13-570870-2

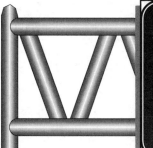

EXPRESSWAYS 1
Activity Workbook
TRAVEL GUIDE

Exit 1 • Meeting and Greeting People

Exit 2 • People and Places

Exit 3 • Getting Around Town

Exit 4 • Housing and Food

Exit 5 • At Work

Exit 6 • Health and Emergencies

Exit 7 • Shopping

Exit 8 • Recreation

APPENDIX

Greet Someone and Introduce Yourself

Student Text Pages 2–3

A. The Right Choice

Circle the correct word.

A. Hello. (My) / Your [1] name is / I'm [2] Sue.

B. Hi. Is / I'm [3] James. Nice to meet / meeting [4] you / too [5].

A. Nice meet / meeting [6] you / too [7], too.

B. Wrong Way!

The greetings are all mixed up! Put the words in the correct order.

A. name Alan. Hello. is My
   <u>Hello. My name is Alan.</u>

B. you. I'm to Carol. Hi. meet Nice
   _____

A. meeting too. Nice you,
   _____

C. Open Road!

Complete the following any way you wish. You meet a new person. What do you say?

....

....

A. Wrong Way!

Put the lines in the correct order.

___ Fine. And you?

___ Fine thanks. I'd like to introduce you to my mother, Mrs. Tanaka.

___ Nice to meet you.

_1_ Hi! How are you?

B. Listen

Listen and circle the word you hear.

1. (husband)   wife
2. mother   father
3. brother   sister
4. wife   sister

5. sister   brother
6. father   mother
7. brother   husband
8. mother   brother

C. Crosswalk

ACROSS

2. I'm Barbara. George is my _____.

3. My name is Michael. Susan is my _____.

5. I'd like to introduce my _____, Jane.

6. And this is my _____, Carlos.

DOWN

1. This is my _____, Mr. Blake.

2. _____ name is Mrs. Blake.

4. Mrs. Blake is my _____.

A. Wrong Way!

Put the lines in the correct order.

____ Chang.

____ And your first name?

____ C-H-A-N-G.

_1_ What's your last name?

____ Richard.

____ Could you spell that, please?

B. Matching Lines

Match the questions and answers.

_c_ **1** What's your last name?   a. J-O-H-N-S-O-N.

____ **2** Could you spell that, please?   b. Fine, thanks.

____ **3** And your first name?   c. Johnson.

____ **4** How are you?   d. John.

C. Listen

Listen and circle the correct name.

1 Tillon   (Dillon)   **6** Mazer   Mazel

2 Ramos   Lamos   **7** Linch   Lynch

3 Barnes   Parnes   **8** Kring   Kling

4 Bassil   Vassil   **9** Wicks   Vicks

5 Baetty   Beatty   **10** Kramer   Cramer

D. The 5th Wheel!

Which one doesn't belong?

1 F   e   ③   v   **4** 3   y   4   6

2 K   p   R   Q   **5** a   m   c   f

3 u   i   b   e   **6** d   v   M   n

3

A. What's the Word?

Complete the conversation.

address	your	13	What's	number	426-7031

A. _____What's_____ ¹ your _____ ²?

B. _____ ³ Main Street.

A. And _____ ⁴ telephone _____ ⁵?

B. _____ ⁶.

B. Matching Lines

Match the questions and answers.

_b_ **1** Drayton.

___ **2** 721-3048.

___ **3** Fine, thanks.

___ **4** 15 Oak Street.

___ **5** D-R-A-Y-T-O-N.

___ **6** Michael.

a. What's your first name?

b. What's your last name?

c. Could you spell that, please?

d. How are you?

e. What's your telephone number?

f. What's your address?

C. Fix the Mistakes!

Correct the mistakes in the following sentences.

1 What your name? _____What's your name?_____

2 What's your telephone street? _____

3 My name Peter Miller. _____

4 My phone number is 15 Elm Street. _____

5 My address is 259-3775. _____

6 Nice meet you. _____

7 Could you spell your last telephone number? _____

D. Listen

Listen and put a check next to the correct answer.

1. ✔ 17 Baker Street.
   ___ 7 Baker Street.

2. ___ 463-9027.
   ___ 473-9072.

3. ___ Are you Mr. Miller?
   ___ Nice to meet you, too.

4. ___ 521-7022.
   ___ 531-7021.

5. ___ 13 Draper Avenue.
   ___ 13 Baker Avenue.

6. ___ Yes. 13.
   ___ No. 31.

7. ___ 3 Bond Road.
   ___ 3 Pond Road.

8. ___ P-O-N-D.
   ___ B-O-N-D.

9. ___ 819-4362.
   ___ 891-4362.

E. Open Road!

Write the name, address, and telephone number of two friends in your address book.

Address Book

Name...

Address..

Telephone number..

Name...

Address..

Telephone number..

Tell Where You're From

A. What's the Question?

Complete the conversation.

Where are you from?   Are you from Rio?   What's your name?

A. _____ *What's your name?* _____

B. Sylvia.

A. _____

B. Brazil.

A. Oh. _____

B. No. I'm from Sao Paulo.

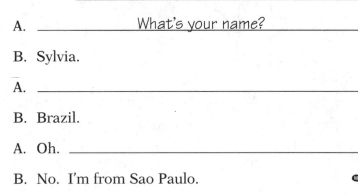

B. Listen

Listen and choose the correct answer.

1. a.) Susan.
   b. Canada.

2. a. Canada.
   b. No. I'm from Canada.

3. a. No. I'm Susan.
   b. No. I'm from Montreal.

4. a. Fine, thank you.
   b. Nice to meet you.

5. a. 15 School Street.
   b. I'm from England.

6. a. Yes. I'm from London.
   b. No. I'm from London.

7. a. Yes. I'm from Tokyo.
   b. Yes. I'm Kenji.

8. a. Japan.
   b. Takahana.

9. a. No. I'm from Tokyo.
   b. No. I'm Kenji.

10. a. Hi. I'm Tom.
    b. Are you David?

11. a. 18 Park Street.
    b. I'm from California.

12. a. No. I'm from Los Angeles.
    b. No. I'm from San Francisco.

C. The Right Choice

Circle the correct word.

1. | His / **He's** | from New York. | His / He | last name is Robertson.

Boston *Jones*

2. | I'm / My | from Boston. | My / I | telephone number is 648-2121.

San Francisco *785-3323*

3. | Our / We | last name is Lopez. | Our / We're | from Mexico.

4. | Their / They're | from Russia. | Their / They | father is Mr. Grinkov.

5. | Her / She's | from Miami. | Her / She's | my sister.

6. | You're / Your | from Chicago. | You / Your | first name is William.

A. What's the Line?

Put a check next to the correct line.

1 Hello. My name is Linda Richmond.

___ Hello. Nice meeting you.
✔ Hello. I'm Louis Livermore.

2 Are you American?

___ Yes, I am. I'm from Dallas. How about you?
___ Yes, I'm Louis. I'm from Dallas. How about you?

3 I'm Canadian. I'm from Montreal.

___ Where are you from?
___ Nice to meet you.

B. What's the Question?

Complete the conversation.

| What's your nationality? | Are you from Seoul? |
| What's your name? | Where are you from? |

A. Hello. _____What's your name?_____

B. Sung Hee Kim.

A. _____

B. Korea.

A. _____

B. Yes, I am.

A. _____

B. I'm Korean.

C. Crosswalk

Mr. and Mrs. Johnson
England
British
London
576-0024

Oscar Ortega
Mexico
Mexican
Mexico City
6311 Long Street

Janet Ling
China
Chinese
Beijing
789-0566

ACROSS

3. Where is Oscar Ortega from?
6. What's Oscar's address?
7. Their last name is _____.
9. Could you spell Janet's last name?
10. She's from China. She's _____.
11. They're from England. They're _____.

DOWN

1. What's Janet's telephone number?
2. Are Mr. and Mrs. Johnson from Liverpool?
4. Where are Mr. and Mrs. Johnson from?
5. Is Janet from Beijing?
7. Her last name is Ling. What's her first name?
8. Mr. Ortega's first name is _____.

D. Listen

Listen and fill out the form.

> **ExpressWays English School**
> **New Student Information Form**
>
> Name: ___Carlos_____
>   First   Last
>
> Address: _____   Telephone: _____
>   Number   Street
>
> Country: ____Puerto Rico____   City: _____

E. The 5th Wheel!

Which one doesn't belong?

1	mother	brother	wife	(Spain)
2	Carol	David	Rome	Charles
3	too	you	they	we
4	China	France	Haiti	Australian
5	12 Oak Street	13 Park Avenue	325-7861	3 River Road

F. WordRap: *Nice to Meet You*

Listen. Then clap and practice.

JILL: Hi. I'm Jill.
BILL: Hello. I'm Bill.
JILL: Nice to meet you.
BILL: Nice to meet you.

ANN: Hi. I'm Ann.
FRAN: Hello. I'm Fran.
ANN: Nice to meet you.
FRAN: Nice to meet you.

JILL: Bill, this is Phil.
BILL: Hi, Phil. I'm Bill.
PHIL: Nice to meet you.
BILL: Nice to meet you.

ANN: Fran, this is Dan.
FRAN: Hi, Dan. I'm Fran.
DAN: Nice to meet you.
FRAN: Nice to meet you.

G. What's the Word?

Complete the following.

I'm	He's	She's	you	They're
My	His	Her	your	Their

_____My_____ [1] name is Oscar. _____ [2] from Bogota. _____ [3] Colombian.

I'd like you to meet my mother and father. _____ [4] names are Alberto and Maria. _____ [5] from Italy. _____ [6] Italian.

This is my husband. _____ [7] from Haiti. _____ [8] name is Roger.

This is my sister. _____ [9] from New York. _____ [10] address is 1201 Third Avenue.

And how about you? What's _____ [11] name? Where are _____ [12] from? What's _____ [13] nationality?

H. Open Road!

Introduce your family.

....

....

....

Call Directory Assistance

Student Text Pages 18–19

A. The Right Choice

Circle the correct word.

A. Directory assistance. (**What** / Where)[1] city?

B. Miami. (I'm / **I'd**)[2] like the (address / number)[3] of James Miller.

A. (Now / **How**)[4] do you (**spell** / tell)[5] that?

B. M-I-L-L-E-R.

A. (What's / **What**)[6] street?

B. Eastern Avenue.

A. Just a (**moment** / number)[7]. The (husband / **number**)[8] (he's / **is**)[9] 756-3298.

B. What's the Line?

Choose the correct line.

1. Directory assistance.
   a. Your name?
   b.) What city?

2. New York.
   a. I'd like the number of Bob Rios.
   b. I'd like to introduce Bob Rios.

3. How do you spell that?
   a. Rios.
   b. R-I-O-S.

A. What's the Word?

Complete the conversation.

You	Sorry	isn't	Is	Hello	I'm	this	it

A. Hello.

B. _____Hello_____ **1**, Jane?

A. _____ **2** sorry. _____ **3** have the wrong number.

B. _____ **4** _____ **5** 758-2210?

A. No, _____ **6** _____ **7**.

B. Oh. _____ **8**.

B. Fix the Mistakes!

Correct the mistakes in the following sentences.

1 I'd sorry.   _____ I'm sorry. _____

2 It this 457-1986?   _____

3 No, it is.   _____

4 You have wrong number.   _____

C. Open Road!

You have the wrong number. What do you say?

Hello.

....
....
....
....
....
....
....

Hello, ...?

D. Wrong Way!

The questions are all mixed up! Put the words in the correct order.

1 _____Is your mother from France_____ ?
from Is mother France your

2 _____ ?
British   you   Are

3 _____ ?
parents   they   his   Are

4 _____ ?
Robertson   Is   Mary   this

5 _____ ?
Greece   they   from   Are

6 _____ ?
Avenue   Belleview   Am   I   on

7 _____ ?
436-6879   Is   number   your

8 _____ ?
you   his   Are   father

9 _____ ?
their   Is   mother   she

10 _____ ?
your   he   Is   brother

E. Matching Lines

Match the questions and answers.

_e_ **1** Are you and your husband from Canada?   a. No, they aren't.

___ **2** Are you in Paris?   b. No, it isn't.

___ **3** Is she your sister?   c. No, I'm not.

___ **4** Am I Australian?   d. No, she isn't.

___ **5** Is your address 5 Main Street?   e. No, we aren't.

___ **6** Is he Mexican?   f. No, you aren't.

___ **7** Are Mr. and Mrs. Lee your parents?   g. No, he isn't.

F. Listen

Listen and choose the correct answer.

1 a. She's from Osaka.   (b.) She isn't from Osaka.

2 a. They're Canadian.   b. They aren't Canadian.

3 a. 742-1980 is a wrong number.   b. 742-1980 isn't a wrong number.

4 a. His name is Marco.   b. His name is Pablo.

5 a. This person is on Third Avenue.   b. This person is on Myrtle Avenue.

6 a. Maria and Franco are their sister and father.   b. Maria and Franco are their mother and father.

A. The Right Choice

Circle the correct word.

A. Hello. This [are / **is**]¹ Bill. [Is / Am]² Marge there?

B. No, she [isn't / is]³ . [Her / She's]⁴ at the bank.

A. Oh, I [she / see]⁵ . I'll [call / am]⁶ back later. Thank you.

B. Crosswalk

ACROSS

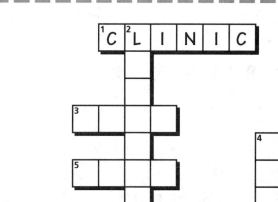

DOWN

15

C. The 5th Wheel!

Which one doesn't belong?

1	avenue	street	(city)	road
2	aren't	is	am	are
3	what	where	how	is
4	I'm not	we're	he isn't	they aren't
5	bank	supermarket	number	park
6	Thank you.	I'm sorry.	Just a moment.	they
7	at school	at the bank	at the clinic	at the library
8	you're	she	he's	it's

D. Listen

Listen and circle the place you hear.

1	(supermarket)	laundromat	4	laundromat	library
2	park	bank	5	post office	school
3	library	clinic	6	park	school

E. Open Road!

Complete these conversations any way you wish.

A. Hello. This is .... Is Betty there?

B. ....

....

A. ....

....

A. Hello. This .... Are Tom and Jim there?

B. ....

....

A. ....

....

A. Wrong Way!

Put the lines in the correct order.

____ I'm going to the mall.

____ Fine. And you?

____ Nice seeing you, too.

____ To the bank. How about you?

__1_ Hi! How are you today?

____ Fine, thanks. Where are you going?

____ Well, nice seeing you.

B. The Right Choice

Circle the correct word.

1 A. Where (are **is**) Harry going?
B. (You're He's) going to the post office.

2 A. Where (is are) John and Robert going?
B. (He's They're) going to the airport.

3 A. Where (are is) Alice going?
B. (He's She's) going to the movies.

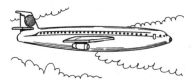

4 A. Where (is are) the airplane going?
B. (It's He's) going to Beijing.

5 A. Where (is are) you going?
B. (I'm You're) going to the museum.

6 A. Where (is are) you and your friend going?
B. (I'm We're) going to the mall.

17

A. Matching Lines

Match the questions and answers.

_c_ **1** What's Linda doing?

____ **2** What are you and Tim doing?

____ **3** What's Michael doing?

____ **4** What are you doing?

____ **5** What am I doing?

____ **6** What are Mr. and Mrs. Ortega doing?

a. He's walking the dog.

b. You're dancing.

c. She's fixing her car.

d. I'm studying English.

e. They're making breakfast.

f. We're cleaning our room.

B. What's the Question?

1 What ____are they____ doing? — They're making breakfast.

2 What's _____? — He's doing his homework.

3 _____ doing? — She's walking the dog.

4 _____ you _____? — I'm looking for my contact lens.

5 _____? — They're doing their exercises.

6 _____? — We're brushing our teeth.

7 _____ I _____? — I think you're dancing.

C. What's the Word?

Complete the sentences.

my	his	her	its	our	your	their

1. Mr. Gomez is looking for ____his____ contact lens.
2. Billy and Bobby are brushing _____ teeth.
3. Mrs. Jenkins is fixing _____ bicycle.
4. The dog is eating _____ dinner.
5. You're cleaning _____ room!
6. I'm combing _____ hair.
7. We're fixing _____ car.
8. My sister is doing _____ homework.

D. Listen

Listen and choose the correct answer.

1. (a.) She's fixing her car. b. She's fixing her bicycle.
2. a. He's doing his exercises. b. He's doing his homework.
3. a. She's walking the dog. b. She's washing the dog.
4. a. He's looking for his contact lens. b. He's looking for his car.
5. a. The dog is eating lunch. b. The dog is eating dinner.
6. a. They're washing their dishes. b. They're brushing their teeth.
7. a. He's cleaning his hair. b. He's combing his hair.
8. a. They're cleaning their apartment. b. They aren't cleaning their apartment.

E. Open Road!

Call a friend. What's your friend doing? Write the telephone conversation.

....
....
....
....
....
....

19

A. Wrong Way!

Put the lines in the correct order.

____ Oh, okay. I'll call back later.

____ Pretty good. How about you?

____ Good-bye.

__1__ Hello, Janet? This is Masako.

____ Okay. Listen, I can't talk right now. I'm cooking dinner.

____ Hi. How are you doing?

____ Speak to you soon.

B. Listen

Listen and check the activities you hear.

What are they doing?

____ making dinner
✔ fixing my car
✔ eating dinner
____ washing dishes
____ cooking dinner
✔ feeding the baby

1

____ walking the dog
____ washing the dishes
____ feeding the baby
____ brushing his teeth
____ cleaning the garage
____ studying

2

Where are they going?

____ to school
____ to the mall
____ to the movies
____ to the supermarket
____ to the clinic
____ to the zoo

3

____ to the post office
____ to the movies
____ to the supermarket
____ to the airport
____ to the museum
____ to Miami

4

C. The Right Choice

Circle the correct word.

1. She's combing her (room (hair)).
2. Are they walking the (school   dog)?
3. Is Peter at the (there   supermarket)?
4. He's doing his (exercises   busy).
5. Where are you (doing   going)?

6. What are you (going   doing)?
7. I'm going to the (mall   teeth).
8. We're making (homework   lunch).
9. She's feeding the (dishes   baby).
10. They're at the (park   Paris).

D. WordRap: *Wrong Number!*

Listen. Then clap and practice.

ALL: Wrong number! Wrong number! Wrong number! Wrong number!

A. Hello.
B. Hello.
A. Is Ted there?
B. Ted?
   There's no Ted here.
A. No Ted?
B. No Ted.

A. Hello.
B. Hello.
A. Is Fred there?
B. Fred?
   There's no Fred here.
A. No Fred?
B. No Fred.

A. Hello.
B. Hello.
A. Is Ed there?
B. Ed?
   There's no Ed here.
A. No Ed?
B. No Ed.

ALL: No Ed! No Ted! No Fred!
     Wrong number! Wrong number! Wrong number! Wrong number!

E. Open Road!

What are these people saying? Write the conversation. Then practice it with a classmate.

F. Matching Lines

Match the questions and answers.

_c_ **1** Are you Canadian?

____ **2** What are you doing?

____ **3** How are you doing?

____ **4** Are your parents here?

a. No, they aren't. They're at the bank.

b. I'm washing my dishes.

c. Yes, I am. I'm from Toronto.

d. Pretty good.

G. Word Search

Find 5 places and 5 family members.

```
M A L L K E R M X F M O K L A
D C B Q I K S Z O A P M Z P W
S L W I F T M A Z L U V P L T
L I B R A R Y A O L U V A L T
E N C L I N R X O V P Q I G J
C I P T Z P I L G K C U R P A
H C Z O P A R E N D Q I P O I
B A B Y A R E R B R O T O Z U
W I F Y R L I B R O R T R O N
A I R H E S C N O L Q C T X E
F A T H N C F A T H E R X E L
Q W I C T V C C H E W C L I N
P S U J S W I F E P X T Y O L
Z I B A B C K G R L O Z M A H
```

Places

_____ mall _____

_____

_____

_____

_____

Family Members

_____

_____

_____

_____

_____

22

Describe the Location of Places in the Community

Student Text
Pages 34–39

A. Wrong Way!

Put the lines in the correct order.

___ On River Road?

___ Yes. There's a post office on River Road.

___ Yes. It's on River Road, across from the mall.

_1_ Excuse me. Is there a post office nearby?

___ Thank you.

B. The Right Choice

Circle the correct words.

A.   (Is there)¹ a drug store nearby?
     Is it

B. Yes.   Is there² a drug store   in³ Oak Street.
           There's   on

A.   There's⁴ a movie theater nearby?
     Is there

B. Yes. It's on Pine Street,   on⁵   the park.
                                across from

A.   It's⁶ a bank nearby?
     Is there

B. Yes. There's a bank   next to⁷   the clinic.
                           next

C. What's the Location?

Answer the questions below based on the map.

next to	on	across from	around the corner from	between

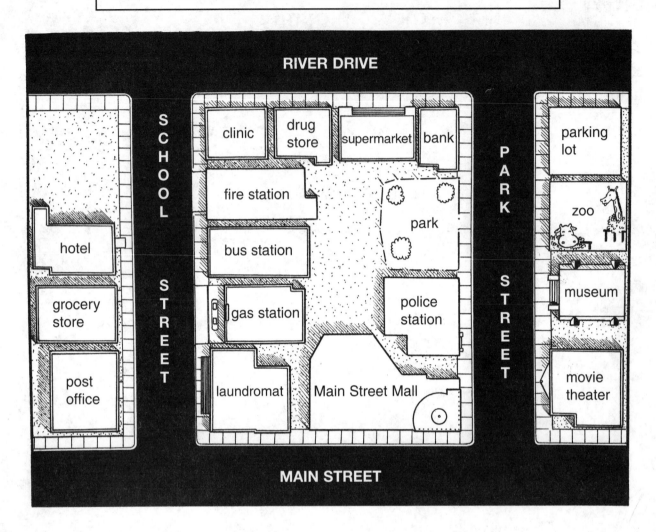

1 The bus station is on School Street, ____across from____ the hotel.

2 The zoo is on Park Street, _____ the museum and the parking lot.

3 The laundromat is on Main Street, _____ the gas station.

4 The police station is _____ Park Street, next to the park.

5 The supermarket is on River Drive, _____ the drug store and the bank.

6 The clinic is _____ the drug store.

7 The Main Street Mall is _____ Main Street.

8 The park is _____ the zoo.

9 The gas station is _____ School Street.

10 The museum is _____ the movie theater.

11 The grocery store is _____ the hotel and the post office.

D. Listen

Listen and circle the letter for each place.

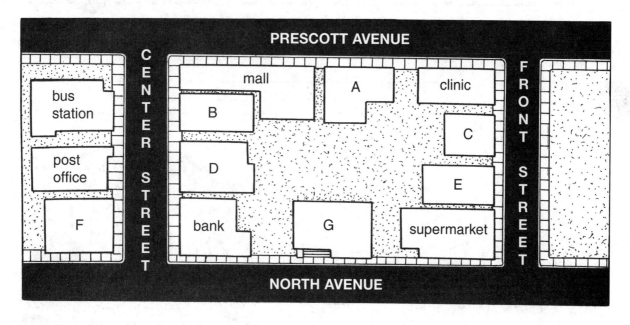

PRESCOTT AVENUE

bus station

post office

F

CENTER STREET

mall

B

D

bank

A

G

clinic

C

E

supermarket

FRONT STREET

NORTH AVENUE

1	Where is the hotel?	Ⓐ	B	C	D	E	F	G
2	Where is the hospital?	A	B	C	D	E	F	G
3	Where is the drug store?	A	B	C	D	E	F	G
4	Where is the school?	A	B	C	D	E	F	G
5	Where is the fire station?	A	B	C	D	E	F	G
6	Where is the parking lot?	A	B	C	D	E	F	G
7	Where is the gas station?	A	B	C	D	E	F	G

E. Open Road!

Write about your neighborhood.

There's a .... in my neighborhood. It's on .... ,
(next to/across from/around the corner from) ....
There's a .... in my neighborhood. It's on .... ,
....
There isn't a .... in my neighborhood.

A. What's the Word?

Complete the conversation.

go	doesn't	it	which	train	Does	goes

A. Excuse me. <u>Does</u> ¹ this _____ ²

_____ ³ to Parkville?

B. No, _____ ⁴ _____ ⁵.

It goes to Centerville.

A. Oh, I see. Tell me, _____ ⁶ train

_____ ⁷ to Parkville?

B. The Number 2 train.

A. Thanks very much.

B. Listen

Listen and choose the correct answer.

1
a. Yes, it does.
(b.) No, it doesn't.

2
a. The Number 60 bus.
b. The Number 16 bus.

3
a. Yes, it does.
b. No, it doesn't.

4
a. Yes, it does.
b. No, it doesn't.

5
a. The Number 13 train.
b. The Number 30 train.

6
a. Yes, it does.
b. No, it doesn't.

7
a. The Number 63 bus.
b. The Number 73 bus.

8
a. Yes, it does.
b. No, it doesn't.

9
a. Yes, it does.
b. No, it doesn't.

10
a. The Number 22 bus.
b. The Number 32 bus.

C. Open Road!

Tell about your community.

Which bus goes to the airport?

....

Which train goes downtown?

....

A. The Right Choice

Circle the correct word.

A. (Is) / Does [1] this the D train?

B. Yes, it does / is [2].

A. Oh, good! It's / I'm [3] on the wrong / right [4] train!

A. Is / Does [5] this bus stop at Baker Street?

B. No, it isn't / doesn't [6].

A. Oops! I'm / It's [7] on the right / wrong [8] bus!

B. Matching Lines

Match the questions and answers.

_c_ 1 Is there a park nearby?   a. No, they aren't.

___ 2 Are they at the bank?   b. Yes, he is

___ 3 Which bus goes to the mall?   c. Yes, there is.

___ 4 Is this the bus to Boston?   d. To the park.

___ 5 Are you going downtown?   e. The Number 52 bus.

___ 6 Does this bus go to the park?   f. No, I'm not.

___ 7 Is he from Seoul?   g. No, it isn't.

___ 8 Where are you going?   h. No, it doesn't.

C. Listen

Listen and complete the bus schedule.

hotel	park
library	theater
mall	train station
museum	zoo

Riverdale Bus Schedule

Bus Number 64	Bus Number 16	Bus Number 54
From: *Park Street bus station*	From: *downtown*	From: *airport*
To: • _____mall_____	To: • _____	To: • _____
• _____	• _____	• _____
• *airport*	• _____	• _____
	• *hospital*	

D. WordRap: *Get on the Bus, Gus!*

Listen. Then clap and practice.

Gus, Gus! Get on the bus!
Get on the bus, Gus!

Jane, Jane! Get on the train!
Get on the train, Jane!

Wayne, Wayne! Get on the plane!
Get on the plane, Wayne!

Gus, Gus! This is your bus!
This is your bus, Gus!

Jane, Jane! This is your train!
This is your train, Jane!

Wayne! Wayne! This is your plane!
This is your plane, Wayne!

This is your bus, Gus!
This is your train, Jane!
This is your plane, Wayne!

A. Wrong Way!

Put the lines in the correct order.

____ I'm sorry. Could you please repeat that?

____ The bank? Yes. Walk THAT way. The bank is on the right, next to the supermarket.

_1_ Excuse me. Can you tell me how to get to the bank?

____ Thank you.

____ All right. Walk THAT way. The bank is on the right, next to the supermarket.

B. Listen

Look at the map and listen to the directions. If the directions are correct, write **C**. If they are incorrect, write **I**.

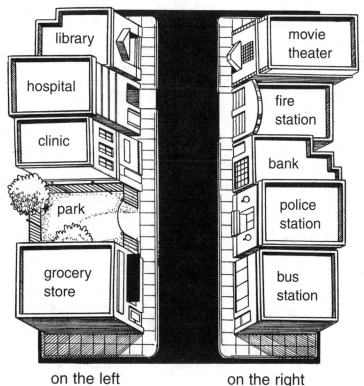

on the left   on the right

 1 ___I___   3 _____   5 _____

 2 ___C___   4 _____   6 _____

A. What's the Word?

Complete the conversation.

look for	Walk	got	get	tell	on	turn	blocks

A. Excuse me. Can you please ____tell____ [1] me how to _____ [2] to the supermarket?

B. Yes. _____ [3] THAT way to Main Street and _____ [4] right.

A. Uh-húh.

B. Then, go two _____ [5] to Stewart Road.

A. Okay.

B. Then, turn left _____ [6] Stewart Road and _____ [7] the supermarket on the right. Have you _____ [8] that?

A. Yes. Thank you very much.

B. What's the Question?

Complete the conversations.

Is there a shopping mall nearby?	Where's the laundromat?
Can you tell me how to get to the bank?	Does this train go downtown?

1. A. ___Where's the laundromat?___
   B. It's on Baker Street, around the corner from Cinema City.

2. A. _____
   B. No, it goes uptown.

3. A. _____
   B. Yes, there is. It's on Parker Street, across from the zoo.

4. A. _____
   B. Yes. Walk THAT way. It's on the left, next to the parking lot.

A. The Right Choice

Circle the correct word.

A. Excuse me. [**Is** / (**Can**)]¹ you tell [**me** / **you**]² how to [**get off** / **get to**]³ the Capital Theater?

B. Sure. [**Take** / **Go**]⁴ the Main Street bus and [**turn left on** / **get off at**]⁵ Day Street.

A. [**I sorry** / **I'm sorry**]⁶ . [**Did** / **Do**]⁷ you say the Main Street bus?

B. Yes. That's [**right** / **wrong**]⁸ .

A. And [**how** / **where**]⁹ do I get off?

B. [**To** / **At**]¹⁰ Day Street.

A. Thanks very much.

B. Matching Lines

Match the lines.

_b_ **1** I'm sorry. _____?   a. is the parking garage

___ **2** Did you say _____?   b. Could you please repeat that

___ **3** Where _____?   c. Bus Number 15 or Bus Number 50

A. Listen

Listen and label the correct places.

| park | zoo | mall | hotel | drug store |

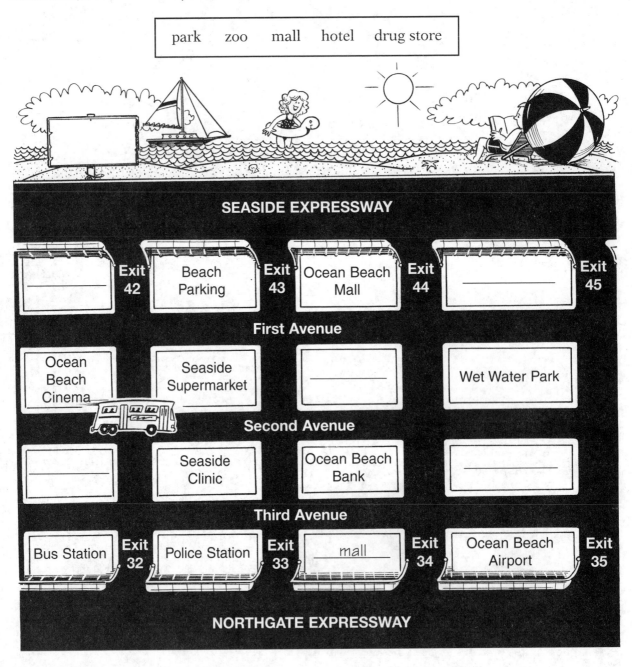

SEASIDE EXPRESSWAY

| Exit 42 | Beach Parking | Exit 43 | Ocean Beach Mall | Exit 44 | _____ | Exit 45 |

First Avenue

Ocean Beach Cinema

Seaside Supermarket

_____

Wet Water Park

Second Avenue

_____

Seaside Clinic

Ocean Beach Bank

_____

Third Avenue

| Bus Station | Exit 32 | Police Station | Exit 33 | mall | Exit 34 | Ocean Beach Airport | Exit 35 |

NORTHGATE EXPRESSWAY

B. Where Do I Live?

I'm in my apartment. Take Exit 32 to get to my apartment. There's a supermarket and a clinic in my neighborhood. My apartment is across from the Ocean Beach Cinema. I live on _____.

C. The 5th Wheel!

Which one doesn't belong?

1	next to	across from	(walk)	between
2	twenty	sixty	ninety	first
3	airport	bus station	train station	hospital
4	expressway	plane	ship	boat
5	is	does	do	doesn't
6	avenue	exit	street	road
7	Take	Get off at	Turn left	I'm sorry
8	third	fifty	second	fourth
9	What	Is there	Where	How

D. Fill It In!

Fill in the correct answer.

1 Is there a theater _____?
 a. neighborhood
 (b.) nearby

2 Take the bus and _____ Fifth Avenue.
 a. got off at
 b. get off at

3 Oh, good! _____.
 a. I'm on the wrong bus.
 b. I'm on the right bus.

4 _____ do I get to the gas station?
 a. How
 b. What

5 _____ are you doing?
 a. Where
 b. What

6 _____ are you going?
 a. Where
 b. What

7 Did you _____ the First Avenue bus?
 a. tell
 b. say

8 Does this _____ stop at Park Street?
 a. bus
 b. plane

9 The museum is next _____ the park.
 a. from
 b. to

10 The hotel is _____ Parker Street.
 a. in
 b. on

11 Have you _____ that?
 a. got
 b. get

A. Open Road!

Answer these questions.

1 What's your name?

....

2 What's your address?

....

3 Where are you from?

....

4 What's your telephone number?

....

B. Fill It In!

Fill in the correct answer.

1 Peter is my _____.
   a. wife
   b. American
   c. brother ⊙

2 My sister isn't here. _____ at the bank.
   a. They're
   b. He's
   c. She's

3 I'm fixing my _____.
   a. address
   b. today
   c. bicycle

4 Timmy is at the library. He's _____.
   a. studying
   b. fixing
   c. going

5 We're _____ our homework.
   a. cleaning
   b. doing
   c. watching

6 _____ three blocks and turn right.
   a. Go
   b. Going
   c. Goes

7 _____ this plane go to Denver?
   a. Is
   b. Does
   c. Is there

8 _____ are you doing?
   a. Where
   b. What
   c. Can

9 I'm going _____ the park.
   a. at
   b. for
   c. to

10 _____ Melissa and Janet there?
   a. Am
   b. Is
   c. Are

11 _____ this bus stop at the mall?
   a. Are
   b. Does
   c. Is

12 _____ your daughter doing?
   a. What
   b. Where
   c. What's

C. What's the Word?

Complete the sentences.

1. ___How___ are you?   I'm fine.
2. _____ Patty doing?   She's studying.
3. _____ are they going?   To the beach.
4. _____ do I get to the expressway?   Drive that way.
5. _____ are they doing?   They're watching TV.

6. Where _____ this bus go?
7. Where _____ he?
8. Where _____ you going?
9. Where _____ this train stop?
10. Where _____ I get off?

D. What's the Answer?

Answer the questions.

1. A. Where's Janet?
   B. ___She's at the laundromat.___

2. A. Where are Fred and Timmy?
   B. _____

3. A. What's Harry doing?
   B. _____

4. A. What are you doing?
   B. _____

E. Listen

Listen and write the number you hear.

1. ___56___   3. _____   5. _____   7. _____

2. _____   4. _____   6. _____   8. _____

Identify Rooms in the Home

Student Text
Pages 56–57

A. Wrong Way!

Put the lines in the correct order.

___ Oh, good. Can you describe it?

___ Yes. It has one bedroom, a nice living room, and a very large kitchen.

_1_ We're looking for a one-bedroom apartment uptown.

___ I think I have an apartment for you.

B. Crosswalk

ACROSS

4

6

7

DOWN

1

2

3

5

Crossword answer: 4 Across — KITCHEN

A. The Right Choice

Circle the correct words.

A. Is there a ((dishwasher) shower)¹ in the kitchen?

B. Yes, there is. (There's   There are)² a very nice dishwasher in the (kitchen   bathroom)³.

A. And how many cabinets (is there   are there)⁴ in the kitchen?

B. Hmm. Let me see. I think (there is   there are)⁵ five (cabinets   cabinet)⁶ in the kitchen.

B. What's the Word?

Complete the sentences.

| building | bathroom | kitchen |
| bedroom | fireplace | |

1. We have a very nice shower in our ___bathroom___ .

2. There are five floors in our _____.

3. We have a very nice stove in our _____.

4. There are two large closets in our _____.

5. Our living room has a very nice _____.

C. What's the Word?

Complete the conversation.

| a   are   the   in   Is   there   There's |

A. ____Is____¹ there a shower _____² the bathroom?

B. Yes, _____³ is. _____⁴ _____⁵ large shower in _____⁶ bathroom.

A. And how many closets _____⁷ _____⁸ _____⁹ the bedroom?

B. Hmm. I think _____¹⁰ _____¹¹ two closets _____¹² _____¹³ bedroom.

D. Likely or Unlikely?

Are the following statements "likely" or "unlikely"?

		Likely	*Unlikely*
1	"There's a shower in the kitchen."	_____	✔
2	"There are cabinets in the bedroom."	_____	_____
3	"There are windows in the living room."	_____	_____
4	"There's a closet in the bedroom."	_____	_____
5	"The apartment has a balcony."	_____	_____
6	"There's a stove in the kitchen."	_____	_____
7	"There's an elevator in the building."	_____	_____
8	"There's a fireplace in the bathroom."	_____	_____
9	"The apartment has twelve bedrooms."	_____	_____

E. What's the Answer?

Answer the questions about this apartment.

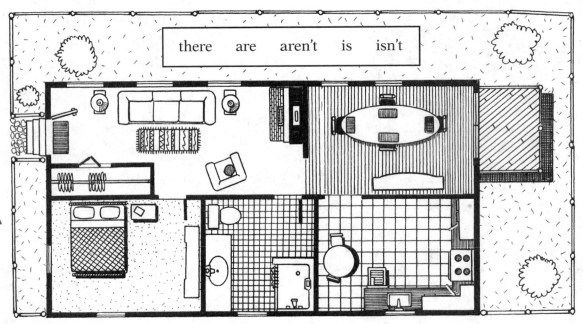

there	are	aren't	is	isn't

1	Is there a fireplace in the living room?	Yes, ___*there is*___.
2	Is there a balcony?	Yes, _____.
3	Are there closets in the bedroom?	No, _____.
4	Are there windows in the living room?	Yes, _____.
5	Is there a refrigerator in the kitchen?	No, _____.
6	Is there a shower in the bathroom?	Yes, _____.
7	Are there cabinets in the kitchen?	Yes, _____.

A. The Right Choice

Circle the correct words.

A.   How many ¹ is the rent?
     (How much)

B.   There's ²
     It's $550 a month.

A.   Does ³ that include   rent ⁴ ?
     Do   utilities

B.   It include ⁵ everything except   elevator ⁶ .
         includes   heat

A.   Hmm. $550 a   moment ⁷ plus heat?
                    month

B.   That's right.   Does you want ⁸ to see the apartment?
                     Do you want

A.   Yes, I think so.

B. Listen

Listen and circle the correct answer.

1. The rent is ($475 ($485)).

2. It includes everything except (parking gas).

3. The parking is ($43 ($34)).

4. This person (wants doesn't want) to see the apartment.

C. Wrong Way!

The questions are all mixed up! Put the words in the correct order.

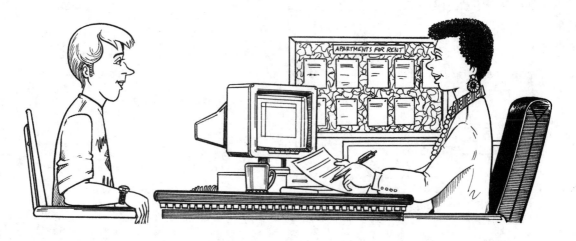

1. _____Is there a dishwasher in the kitchen?_____

a   dishwasher   kitchen?   Is   in   there   the

2. _____

rent?   How   is   the   much

3. _____

include   Does   utilities?   that

4. _____

university?   near   the   it   Is

5. _____

there   patio?   a   Is

6. _____

there?   bedrooms   How   are   many

7. _____

parking   spaces   the   Are   in   there   lot?   parking

D. What's the Answer?

Read the advertisement and answer the questions from Exercise C above.

APARTMENT FOR RENT

2–bedroom apartment,
dishwasher, large living room,
nice balcony, near the park,
free parking in parking lot,
$625 plus gas.

1. _____Yes, there is._____

2. _____

3. _____

4. _____

5. _____

6. _____

7. _____

E. Open Road!

Write about your house or apartment.

My house/apartment has ....

....

It's near ....

I like my house/apartment because ....

....

F. WordRap: *I Have an Apartment*

Listen. Then clap and practice.

I have a new apartment,
A nice new apartment,
With high ceilings
And very low rent.

I have a new apartment,
A nice new apartment,
With three large rooms
And very low rent.

I have a new apartment,
A nice new apartment,
With a wonderful view
And very low rent.

Large rooms!
High ceilings!
Very low rent!

Large rooms!
High ceilings!
Very low rent!

I have an old apartment,
An ugly old apartment,
With low ceilings
And very high rent.

I have an old apartment,
An ugly old apartment,
With three small rooms
And very high rent.

I have an old apartment,
An ugly old apartment,
With no view
And very high rent.

Small rooms!
Low ceilings!
Very high rent!

Small rooms!
Low ceilings!
Very high rent!

A. What's the Word?

Complete the conversation.

this	That	these	those

A. Where do you want _____ this _____ ¹ TV?

B. _____ ² TV? Hmm. Put it in the living room.

A. And how about _____ ³ plants?

B. _____ ⁴ plants? Let me see.
Please put them in the dining room.

B. Crosswalk

this	That	these	those

ACROSS

1 A. Where do you want _____ waterbed? *lamp*
B. That waterbed? Put it in the bedroom.

3 A. And _____ bicycles? *chairs*

4 B. _____ bicycles? Put them on
the balcony.

DOWN

1 A. Where do you want these pictures? *apples*
B. _____ pictures? Put them on the table.

2 A. And this crib? *pineapple watermelon*
B. _____ crib? Put it in the bedroom.

3 A. And how about _____ rug?
B. Please put it in the dining room.

rug

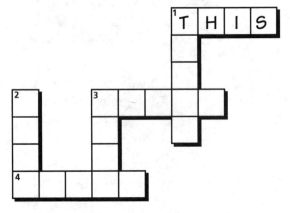

Crossword: 1 Across/Down starting with T-H-I-S

C. Listen

Listen and circle the word you hear.

1 this (these)

2 those these

3 that those

4 those these

5 that this

6 these this

7 that those

8 this that

42

D. Wrong Way!

Put the lines in the correct order.

1 ___ Hmm. Please put them in the living room.

___ Let me see. Please put it in the bedroom.

_1_ Where do you want these pictures?

___ And how about this rug?

2 ___ Let me see. You want the pictures in the living room, the rug in the bedroom, and the TV in the kitchen. How about these plants?

___ What about this TV?

___ Please put them on the balcony.

___ Please put it in the kitchen.

E. Word Search

Can you find 9 things that go in the house?

(P	I	C	T	U	R	E)	P	H	B	Y	O	B	M	C
D	O	B	A	H	F	S	O	F	A	F	S	E	P	W
S	L	W	I	F	T	M	A	Z	L	U	V	D	L	T
W	A	T	E	R	B	E	D	O	P	U	B	A	L	V
E	M	C	L	I	N	R	X	O	V	P	Q	I	G	J
C	P	P	T	Z	P	I	L	G	K	C	U	R	P	A
H	C	Z	O	P	A	R	E	N	D	Q	I	P	O	I
L	I	C	I	N	G	M	O	O	R	O	T	Y	B	U
W	I	H	V	R	L	I	B	R	O	R	T	R	O	N
A	I	A	H	E	S	C	N	O	P	Q	C	T	J	E
B	B	I	L	B	I	C	Y	C	L	E	B	M	R	L
T	A	R	B	N	M	T	A	B	L	E	N	V	I	N

43

A. What's the Word?

Complete the conversation.

There	An	any	some	What	on	there	aren't

A. _____ What _____ ¹ are you looking for?

B. _____ ² orange.

A. I'm afraid _____ ³ _____ ⁴ more oranges.

B. _____ ⁵ aren't?

A. No. I'll get _____ ⁶ more when I go to the supermarket.

B. Fill It In!

Fill in the correct answer.

1 What are you _____ for?
    a. doing
    (b.) looking

2 I'm looking for _____.
    a. a tomato
    b. an tomato

3 How about _____?
    a. an banana
    b. a banana

4 Do you want some more _____?
    a. elevator
    b. eggs

5 I'm afraid there aren't _____.
    a. any more apples
    b. some more apples

6 _____ aren't?
    a. This
    b. There

7 I'll get _____.
    a. some more
    b. any more

8 Do you want _____?
    a. a apple
    b. an apple

9 Is there _____?
    a. a dishwasher
    b. an dishwasher

10 I'm looking for an _____.
    a. egg
    b. cookie

11 There aren't any more _____.
    a. orange
    b. oranges

12 I'll get some at the _____.
    a. kitchen
    b. supermarket

Identify More Food Items

A. Wrong Way!

Put the lines in the correct order.

____ I'm afraid there isn't any more coffee.

____ No. I'll get some more when I go to the supermarket.

____ Coffee.

__1__ What are you looking for?

____ There isn't?

B. Listen

Listen and circle the word you hear.

1	is	(isn't)	4	isn't	aren't	7	isn't	aren't
2	isn't	aren't	5	are	aren't	8	are	aren't
3	are	aren't	6	is	isn't	9	aren't	isn't

C. Crosswalk

ACROSS

DOWN

A. Listen

Listen to the conversations and complete the missing information.

A. Excuse me. Where are the potatoes?

B. They're in Aisle __3__ **1**.

A. I'm sorry. Did you say _____ **2**?

B. No. _____ **3**.

A. Oh. Thank you.

A. Excuse me. Where's the yogurt?

B. It's in Aisle _____ **4**.

A. I'm sorry. Did you say _____ **5**?

B. No. _____ **6**.

A. Oh. Thank you.

B. Which Group?

Write the words in the correct group.

apples	butter	potatoes	peaches	yogurt
bread	lettuce	bananas	cookies	cheese

Baked Goods	Dairy Products	Fruits	Vegetables
_____	_____	_apples_	_____
_____	_____	_____	_____
	_____	_____	

C. Scrambled Foods!

Put the letters in the correct order.

1 n e r o g a _o r a n g e_

2 n a b a n a _____

3 f e c o f e _____

4 k i l m _____

5 c e r i _____

6 p a l e p _____

7 u f t o _____

8 g e g s _____

Exchange Information

A. The 5th Wheel!

Which one doesn't belong?

1	ice cream	(lettuce)	milk	yogurt
2	heat	electricity	rent	gas
3	parking lot	dishwasher	refrigerator	shower
4	crib	sofa	elevator	lamp
5	a cake	an apple	a cookie	a carrot
6	university	peach	beach	hospital
7	rice	raisins	bananas	oranges
8	fourth	four hundred	six hundred fifty	two hundred fifteen
9	cabbage	pork	bean sprouts	carrots
10	bedroom	kitchen	bathroom	patio

B. What's the Response?

Choose the correct response.

1. This bread is delicious!
   a. I'm sorry.
   (b.) I'm glad you like it.

2. These cookies are excellent!
   a. I'm glad you like it.
   b. Thanks for saying so.

3. I think I have an apartment for you!
   a. Good-bye.
   b. Oh, good!

4. Please put that table over there.
   a. Okay.
   b. I'm lost!

5. $800 a month plus heat?
   a. Thank you.
   b. That's right.

6. What's in this cake?
   a. Let me think.
   b. Thank you very much.

7. Can you describe the apartment?
   a. It's very large.
   b. Okay so far?

8. Does that include heat?
   a. That's wrong.
   b. No, it doesn't.

9. Could you repeat that?
   a. Thank you for saying so.
   b. All right.

10. I'm sorry. Did you say Aisle "C"?
    a. Yes. "3."
    b. No. "3."

Tell About Occupations

Student Text Pages 74–75

A. The Right Choice

Circle the correct word.

A. [How / (What)]¹ do you do?

B. [I'm / I do]² a salesperson.

A. Oh, really? [Which / What]³ [does / do]⁴ you sell?

B. I [teach / sell]⁵ jewelry.

B. Matching Lines

What do they do?

_d_	**1**	teacher	a. "I sell furniture."
___	**2**	architect	b. "I fix stoves."
___	**3**	writer	c. "I assemble VCRs."
___	**4**	repairperson	d. "I teach English."
___	**5**	salesperson	e. "I write novels."
___	**6**	assembler	f. "I design houses."

C. Open Road!

What do YOU do?

....

....

A. Wrong Way!

Put the lines in the correct order.

___ That's interesting. What instrument does he play?

___ He's a musician.

_1_ What does your father do?

___ He plays the violin.

B. The Right Choice

Circle the correct word.

1. Josephine is an assembler. She (assemble (assembles)) toys.
2. My son is a mechanic. He (fix   fixes) cars.
3. I'm a chef. I (work   works) at the Roadside Café.
4. My wife is a teacher. She (teach   teaches) English.
5. My mother and my father are musicians. They (play   plays) the piano and the violin.
6. We're architects. We (design   designs) buildings.

C. Crosswalk

ACROSS

2. I assemble radios. I'm an _____.
5. She fixes VCRs. She's a _____.
7. I fix cars. I'm a _____.

DOWN

1. I guard buildings. I'm a _____.
3. I work at a restaurant. I'm a _____.
4. He designs factories. He's an _____.
6. I play the piano. I'm a _____.

D. Word Search

Can you find 13 occupations?

```
P S S A L E S P E R S O N A L
D C E Q I K S Z O A P M Z D W
S L C I F (B A K E R) U V C E T
M I R R A R Y A O L U V H L T
U N E L I N R X O V P Q E I J
S I T T Z P I L A K C U F V A
I C A O P A R W R I T E R E S
C A R Y A R E R C R O T O R S
I I Y Y R L I B H O R T R Y E
A I R H E S C N I L Q C T P M
N A T H N C F A T H E R X E B
Q R E P A I R P E R S O N R L
P M E C H A N I C P X T Y S E
Z I B A B C K G T L O Z M O R
M W I C T V C C H E W C L N A
T E A C H E R T C R H E T A B
S I S E C U R I T Y G U A R D
G D S C Y T R I D G R A X P A
```

E. Sense or Nonsense?

Do the following "make sense" or are they "nonsense"?

		Sense	*Nonsense*
1	"My brother is a musician. He plays the violin."	✓	
2	"I'm a mechanic. I fix jewelry."		
3	"My husband is a writer. He writes VCRs."		
4	"I'm a teacher. I work at a school."		
5	"I'm a salesperson at the mall."		
6	"I'm a baker. I make delicious cakes."		
7	"My wife is an architect. She designs novels."		
8	"My sister is a bilingual secretary. She only speaks English."		

50

A. The Right Choice

Circle the correct word.

A. Can you teach ((Spanish) cars)¹ ?

B. Yes, I (can't can)². I'm an experienced (mechanic teacher)³.

A. (Is Can)⁴ you speak Bengali?

B. No, I (can can't)⁵. But, I'm sure I (can can't)⁶ learn quickly.

B. Listen

What can Linda do? Listen and circle "can" or "can't."

1	*play the violin*	(can)	can't	7	*fix a car*	can	can't
2	*play the piano*	can	can't	8	*speak Italian*	can	can't
3	*dance*	can	can't	9	*speak French*	can	can't
4	*sing*	can	can't	10	*teach French*	can	can't
5	*write novels*	can	can't	11	*use a computer*	can	can't
6	*fix a radio*	can	can't	12	*design a computer*	can	can't

C. Right or Wrong?

If the sentence is correct, write **C**. If it is incorrect, write **I** and correct it.

1 Maria cans speak Spanish.

  ___I___ ___Maria can speak Spanish.___

2 What languages does they speak?

  _____

3 Where does he work?

  _____

4 She can't dances.

  _____

5 They speak English and Japanese.

  _____

6 He work at the bakery.

  _____

Describe People

Student Text Pages 80–81

A. Listen

Listen and write the number under the correct person.

_____ _____ 1 _____

_____ _____ _____ _____

B. Matching Lines

Match the questions and answers.

_d_ **1** Is John tall?

____ **2** Is your hair red?

____ **3** What does your sister look like?

____ **4** Is her hair curly?

____ **5** Is your wife short?

____ **6** What does your husband do?

____ **7** What do you do?

____ **8** Where does Paul work?

____ **9** Is Mr. Davis heavy?

a. He's a baker.

b. No. Her hair is straight.

c. I'm a mechanic.

d. Yes. He's very tall.

e. She's average height, with blonde hair.

f. No. He's very thin.

g. He works at We "R" Toys.

h. No. My hair is gray.

i. No. She's tall.

A. What's the Word?

Complete the conversations.

us	them	her	him	it	me

1 A. Am I assembling this radio all right?

B. Yes, you are. You're assembling
___it___ very well.

2 A. Am I shampooing Mrs. Diaz all right?

B. Yes, you are. You're shampooing
_____ very well.

3 A. Does your boss compliment you very often?

B. Yes, she does. She compliments
_____ all the time.

4 A. Does your supervisor meet with you and your co-workers very often?

B. Yes, she does. She meets with _____ every week.

5 A. Am I guarding the president all right?

B. Yes, you are. You're guarding
_____ very well.

6 A. Am I stocking the shelves all right?

B. Yes, you are. You're stocking _____ very well.

B. Listen

Listen and circle the word you hear.

1 (it)   we   **4** him   it   **7** me   him

2 me   us   **5** him   her   **8** him   her

3 we   me   **6** them   him   **9** them   him

C. What's the Response?

Choose the correct response.

1 Am I giving this presentation all right?
    a. You're giving it very well.
    b. I'm glad you like it.

2 Is her hair straight?
    a. Yes, it's straight.
    b. No, it's straight.

3 I think I have an apartment for you.
    a. It's excellent.
    b. Can you describe it?

4 What does he deliver?
    a. He delivers downtown.
    b. He delivers waterbeds.

5 Do you sell VCRs?
    a. No, I repair them.
    b. No, I repair it.

6 Can you teach Chemistry?
    a. Yes, I can teach him.
    b. Yes, I can teach it.

7 Do you miss us?
    a. We miss you very much.
    b. You miss us very much.

8 Does your boss compliment the workers?
    a. She compliments them all the time.
    b. She compliments you all the time.

D. WordRap

Listen. Then clap and practice.

A Terrible Place to Work!

Don't apply for a job in that place.
It's a terrible place to work!
The hours are long.
The breaks are short.
The pay is poor.
The boss is mean.
The people are nasty.
The work is dull.
It's a terrible place to work!

A Wonderful Place to Work!

You should apply for a job in that place.
It's a wonderful place to work!
The hours are short.
The breaks are long.
The pay is good.
The boss is kind.
The people are nice.
The work is fun.
It's a wonderful place to work!

Tell About Everyday Activities

Student Text Pages 84–85

A. Wrong Way!

Put the lines in the correct order.

____ Hmm. What day is it?

____ I'm afraid I'm busy. I work out at the gym on Wednesday.

____ It's Wednesday.

_1_ Are you busy after work today?

B. What's the Order?

Put the days in the correct order.

____ Tuesday

____ Friday

_1_ Sunday

____ Thursday

____ Monday

____ Wednesday

____ Saturday

C. Matching Lines

Match the lines.

_f_ ① I work out at the ____.   a. lessons

____ ② I take a computer ____.   b. hospital

____ ③ My grandfather lives in a very nice ____.   c. class

____ ④ I take guitar ____.   d. nursing home

____ ⑤ I coach my son's baseball ____.   e. team

____ ⑥ Every Saturday I volunteer at the ____.   f. gym

D. Listen

Listen and circle the word you hear.

① Sunday   (Monday)   ④ class   lesson

② grandmother   grandfather   ⑤ team   gym

③ Thursday   Tuesday   ⑥ Saturday   Friday

E. Fill It In!

Ben is a very busy person. Look at his schedule and complete the following.

| Sunday | Monday | Tuesday | Wednesday | Thursday | Friday | Saturday |

---

take violin lessons		work out at the gym		volunteer at the hospital
play tennis		go to a computer class		coach his son's soccer team
		visit his grandmother at the nursing home		

On Sunday he __plays tennis_____.

On Monday he _____.

On Tuesday he _____.

On Wednesday he _____.

On Thursday he _____.

On Friday he _____.

On Saturday he _____.

F. What's the Word?

Complete the sentences.

| take | work out | volunteer | go | visit | coach |

1. My son _____takes_____ violin lessons. He's a very good musician.

2. My wife and I _____ to a computer class every Friday after work.

3. My husband _____ our daughter's soccer team.

4. My children _____ their grandparents every weekend.

5. I think it's great that you _____ at the gym every day.

6. My daughter _____ at the local hospital every Wednesday after school.

A. What's the Line?

Complete the conversations.

> Not really. We rarely see each other during the week.
> Not very often. They live far away.
> We usually call them on Saturday evening.
> No. They rarely visit us. We usually visit them.
> Because we both work.
> Never. We always call them.
> Sometimes, but we usually talk to them on the
> telephone.

1 A. How often do you talk to your daughters in Chicago?

B. <u>We usually call them</u>

<u>on Saturday evening.</u>

A. Do they ever call you?

B. _____

_____

2 A. Do you and your girlfriend see each other very often?

B. _____

_____

A. Why?

B. _____

_____

3 A. How often do you see your parents?

B. _____

_____

A. Do you go to visit them?

B. _____

_____

A. Do they ever visit you?

B. _____

_____

B. Fill It In!

Fill in the correct answer.

1 We don't ____ to our grandchildren very often.
    a. see
    b. talk *(circled)*

2 They visit their grandparents very ____.
    a. often
    b. never

3 My boyfriend and I ____ see each other during the week because we're usually busy.
    a. always
    b. rarely

4 ____ often do you write to your uncle in Chicago?
    a. Who
    b. How

5 We ____ call each other on the telephone every Sunday afternoon.
    a. never
    b. usually

6 You can always ____ me on my beeper.
    a. keep
    b. beep

7 Please stay in ____ with us.
    a. touch
    b. telephone

8 I'm really sorry I ____ my friends more often.
    a. see
    b. don't see

9 I often ____ my friend Elizabeth on her car phone.
    a. call
    b. visit

10 We're lucky we both have fax machines because ____ always home to talk on the telephone.
    a. we're
    b. we aren't

C. Listen

Listen and decide if the following statements are true or false.

1 She writes to her parents every day.   ___ True   ✔ False

2 He doesn't see his sister very often.   ___ True   ___ False

3 She speaks to her parents on Saturday or Sunday.   ___ True   ___ False

4 She doesn't have a car phone.   ___ True   ___ False

5 He and his friends are in touch with each other.   ___ True   ___ False

6 He's always at home on Saturday nights.   ___ True   ___ False

7 She sees her grandmother very often.   ___ True   ___ False

8 He usually takes the bus downtown.   ___ True   ___ False

9 He's in touch with his friend Bob.   ___ True   ___ False

10 She often faxes her friends on her fax machine.   ___ True   ___ False

11 There are many ways to keep in touch with Dr. Wu.   ___ True   ___ False

Student Text Pages 88–89

A. Wrong Way!

Put the lines in the correct order.

___ What's your favorite movie?

___ "Rolly Rabbit."

___ I like science-fiction movies.

_1_ What kind of movies do you like?

___ "Creature from Mars!" How about you?

___ I like cartoons. How about you?

B. Sports Crosswalk

ACROSS

DOWN

C. Open Road!

Complete the following about yourself.

1 What sports do you like?

....
....
....

2 What sports can you play?

....
....
....

D. Movie Match

Match the advertisement with the type of movie.

comedy	drama	science fiction movie
western	cartoon	adventure movie

1 "Visit Egypt, Italy, and China to look for a tall, blonde woman!" ___adventure movie___

2 "Ha, ha, ha! Inspector Blouseau is here!" _____

3 "Go to Mars with a short red creature from outer space!" _____

4 "Kids agree! This movie is their favorite!" _____

5 "Visit the West and see your favorite cowboys!" _____

6 "A musician teaches his girlfriend to play the violin, but they lose touch and never see each other again." _____

E. Listen

Listen and circle the correct answer.

1 (sitcoms)   dramas   **4** classical   country

2 cartoons   comedies   **5** "Newstime"   "Zootime"

3 rock   rap   **6** "I Miss You"   "I Meet You"

F. The 5th Wheel!

Which one doesn't belong?

1 baseball   football   hockey   (jazz)

2 sitcoms   comedy movies adventure movies   science-fiction movies

3 rap music   dramas   jazz   country music

4 rock music   talk shows   news   game shows

5 Beethoven   Handel   The Beatles   Brahms

6 program   movie star   performer   sports star

G. What Day Is It?

Unscramble the days of the week.

1 idFary   <u>F r i d a y</u>   **4** arytdSua   _ _ _ _ _ _ _ _

2 hraTydus   _ _ _ _ _ _ _ _   **5** naddesWey   _ _ _ _ _ _ _ _ _

3 odMyna   _ _ _ _ _ _   **6** udynaS   _ _ _ _ _ _

7 What day is missing? _____

H. What's the Line?

Complete the conversations.

| team   movies   music   day of the week   height   fruit   number   vegetable |

1 What's your favorite <u>day of the week</u> ?   I like Friday.

2 What _____ do you like?   I like carrots.

3 Do you like _____?   Yes, I do. I like rap and jazz.

4 What _____ do you like?   I like the Blue Sox.

5 What's your brother's _____?   He's very tall.

6 Do you like to go to the _____?   Yes, I do. I like comedies.

7 What's kind of _____ do you like?   I like oranges.

8 What's your lucky _____?   Fifteen.

Identify Common Ailments

Student Text Pages 92–93

A. Wrong Way!

Put the lines in the correct order.

____ What's the matter?

____ I'm sorry to hear that.

__1__ You know . . . you don't look very well. Are you feeling okay?

____ I have a stomachache.

____ No, not really.

B. What's the Word?

Complete the sentences.

have has	earache toothache sore throat stomachaches headaches backaches

1  Sally ____has____ an ____earache____.

2  Bob and Emma _____ _____.

3  Billy _____ a _____.

4  Betty and Ben _____ _____.

5  We _____ _____.

6  Margaret _____ a _____.

C. Open Road!

This person doesn't feel well. What's the matter with her?

I think she ....

Ask for Recommendations

A. The Right Choice

Circle the correct word.

A. Excuse me. Can you help me?

B. Yes.

A. I (has **have**)¹ a terrible sore throat.
   What (do   are)² you recommend?

B. I (recommends   recommend)³ Breezy
   Throat Lozenges.

A. Breezy Throat Lozenges?

B. Yes.

A. Where can I find (it   them)⁴?

B. (They're   It's)⁵ in Aisle 4 on the bottom shelf.

B. What's the Response?

Choose the correct response.

1 I have an earache. What do you
recommend?
   a. I recommend chicken soup.
   b. I recommend ear drops.

2 Where can I find aspirin?
   a. It's in the front near the
      cash register.
   b. It's on the front near the
      cash register.

3 What do you recommend for a
stomachache?
   a. I recommend strong tea.
   b. I recommend cake and cookies.

4 Excuse me. Can you help me?
   a. What do you recommend?
   b. Yes.

5 Cough syrup is in Aisle 9.
   a. Can you help me?
   b. Thank you.

6 Where can I find them?
   a. They're in Aisle 6 on the left.
   b. It's in Aisle 6 on the left.

7 Where can I find throat lozenges?
   a. It's in Aisle 12 in the
      bottom shelf.
   b. They're in Aisle 12 on the
      bottom shelf.

8 Where can I find Chiller's Cold
Medicine?
   a. It's in Aisle 3 on the top shelf.
   b. They're in Aisle 3 on the top
      shelf.

9 What's the matter?
   a. The cough syrup is on the right.
   b. I have a bad cough.

10 I have a bad backache.
   a. It's in Aisle 5.
   b. I'm sorry to hear that.

C. Listen

Listen to the pharmacist's directions and choose the correct answer.

1. a. on the bottom shelf
   b. on the top shelf ⓑ
2. a. on the middle shelf
   b. on the bottom shelf
3. a. on the middle shelf
   b. on the bottom shelf
4. a. in Aisle 5
   b. in Aisle 9

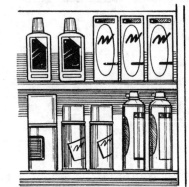

5. a. near the front
   b. near the back
6. a. in the back
   b. on the back
7. a. on the front
   b. in the front
8. a. on the top shelf
   b. on the bottom shelf

D. A Good Idea or Not a Good Idea?

Decide if each of these recommendations is a good idea or is not a good idea.

	A Good Idea	Not a Good Idea
1. Bill recommends ear drops for a sore throat.	_____	✔
2. I recommend aspirin for a headache.	_____	_____
3. I recommend Tummy-Aid Tablets for an earache.	_____	_____
4. My mother recommends chicken soup for a cold.	_____	_____
5. We recommend cough syrup for a stomachache.	_____	_____
6. I recommend a hot shower for a toothache.	_____	_____
7. My sister recommends carrots for a backache.	_____	_____
8. My father recommends Silence Cough Syrup for a bad cough.	_____	_____

E. Wrong Way!

The questions are all mixed up! Put the words in the correct order.

1. _____Where can I find it?_____
   it?   Where   I   find   can

2. _____
   recommend?   do   What   you

3. _____
   me?   help   Can   you

4. _____
   find   I   them?   Where   can

5. _____
   okay?   you   Are   feeling

Make a Doctor's Appointment

A. The Right Choice

Circle the correct word.

A. Doctor's office.

B. Hello. **I'm** / (**This**)¹ is Mr. Blaine. My son **aren't** / **isn't**² **feeling** / **feel**³ very well.

A. **It's** / **What's**⁴ the problem?

B. **His** / **My**⁵ ears are **ring** / **ringing**⁶.

A. I see. Do you want to **has** / **make**⁷ an appointment?

B. Yes, please.

A. **Cans** / **Can**⁸ you **come in** / **comes in**⁹ this afternoon at 4:00?

B. This afternoon at 4:00? Yes. That's **wrong** / **fine**¹⁰. Thank you.

A. See you this afternoon. Good-bye.

B. Mix-Up!

Put the letters in the correct order to find the patient's problem.

The patient has a d b a   h t h c o a t e o.   _bad toothache_

C. Matching Times

Match the times.

<u>h</u> **1** It's three o'clock.

___ **2** It's nine fifteen.

___ **3** It's ten forty-five.

___ **4** It's five o'clock.

___ **5** It's seven thirty.

___ **6** It's two forty-five.

___ **7** It's eight o'clock.

___ **8** It's twelve thirty.

___ **9** It's one fifteen.

___ **10** It's four forty-five.

___ **11** It's six o'clock.

___ **12** It's eleven thirty.

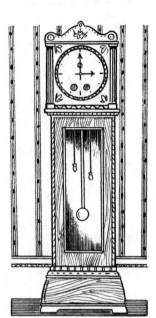

a. 12:30

b. 2:45

c. 11:30

d. 10:45

e. 6:00

f. 1:15

g. 7:30

h. 3:00

i. 8:00

j. 9:15

k. 5:00

l. 4:45

D. Listen

Listen and circle the correct time.

1 7:30   (11:30)   **4** 4:45   5:45   **7** 8:15   3:15

2 12:00   11:00   **5** 12:00   2:00   **8** 6:45   7:45

3 3:15   3:30   **6** 10:45   2:45   **9** 5:30   9:30

E. WordRap: *Medical Advice*

Listen. Then clap and practice.

A. I'm getting a cold.
B. Listen to me. Twice a day take Vitamin C.

A. I have a bad headache. I think it's the weather.
B. Take one or two aspirin. You'll feel a lot better.

A. My lungs still hurt. It's hard to breathe.
B. Go to bed immediately!

A. I'm having trouble with my ear.
B. Try these drops right over here.

A. My throat is sore. My ears are ringing.
B. No flying in planes, no shouting, no singing!

A. I'm feeling tired. I'm gaining weight.
B. Lose ten pounds. It's not too late!

A. What's the Response?

Circle the correct response.

A. I have just one more question.

B. (I agree (All right))¹.

A. Is there a history of heart disease in your family?

B. (No, there isn't   No, I don't)².

A. Okay. I think that's all the information I need for your medical history. The doctor will see you shortly.

B. (Thank you.   Nice meeting you)³.

B. Matching Lines

Match the questions and answers.

__d__ 1 Do you smoke?

____ 2 Are you allergic to anything?

____ 3 Do you drink?

____ 4 Does Maria exercise regularly?

____ 5 What's your son's problem?

____ 6 What's the matter with Bill and Bob?

____ 7 Is there a history of heart disease in your family?

____ 8 Are there any medications you are currently taking?

____ 9 Are you currently having any medical problems?

____ 10 What do you recommend for a sore throat?

a. He has an earache.

b. I always recommend lozenges.

c. Yes, I am. I have a sore throat.

d. No. I never smoke.

e. They have backaches.

f. No, I don't.

g. No, there aren't.

h. No, she doesn't.

i. Yes. I'm allergic to penicillin.

j. Yes, there is.

C. Mystery Malady!

Put the letters in the correct order to discover the mystery malady.

r t e h a   s a e i d e s   _ _ _ _ _   _ _ _ _ _ _ _

D. What's the Response?

Choose the correct response.

1 Tell me, are you allergic to anything?
    a. No, I'm not. *(circled)*
    b. Yes, you do.

2 Is there a history of lung disease in your family?
    a. Yes, they do.
    b. Yes, there is.

3 Are you currently taking any medication?
    a. Yes, you do.
    b. No, I'm not.

4 Do you have any other problems?
    a. No, I don't.
    b. No, there isn't.

5 Do you still have a bad toothache?
    a. Yes, there is.
    b. Yes, I do.

6 Tell me, does your foot hurt very badly?
    a. No, they don't.
    b. Yes, it does.

7 Is your son still feeling dizzy?
    a. Yes, he is.
    b. No, he doesn't.

8 Are your daughter's ears still ringing?
    a. Yes, she is.
    b. Yes, they are.

E. Fix the Mistakes!

Correct the mistakes in the following sentences.

1 I allergic to aspirin.   _I'm allergic to aspirin._

2 There a history of heart disease in our family.   _____

3 Does you have any more questions?   _____

4 Frank doesn't takes any medication.   _____

5 We doesn't have any allergies.   _____

6 I'm not feel well today.   _____

F. Open Road!

Fill in the following medical chart with information about yourself.

Personal Medical Chart

I'm allergic to ....

In my family there's a history of ....

I'm currently taking the following medications:

....

....

A. What's the Line?

Complete these instructions.

| at | off | up | on |

1. Take _off_ your shirt.
2. Sit ____ the table.
3. Roll ____ your sleeve.
4. Look ____ the ceiling.
5. Lie ____ your back.

B. Likely or Unlikely?

Which of these things did the doctor say? Check "likely" or "unlikely."

		Likely	Unlikely
1	"Say 'a-a-h.'"	✔	
2	"Hold your breath."		
3	"Touch the ceiling."		
4	"Sit on your shirt."		
5	"Raise your right arm."		
6	"Hold your toes."		
7	"Touch your toes."		
8	"Stand up on the table."		
9	"Lie on your elbow."		
10	"Take off your shirt."		
11	"Look at your eye."		

69

Receive a Doctor's Medical Advice

A. Wrong Way!

Put the lines in the correct order.

____ I suggest you use it daily.

____ My gums?

____ I understand. Thank you for the advice.

____ I see.

_1_ I'm concerned about your gums.

____ Yes. You should use dental floss.

B. Listen

Listen to the conversations and answer the questions.

Conversation 1

1. The doctor is concerned about the patient's ____.
   a. weight
   b. blood pressure ⟵ (circled)

2. The patient ____ change his diet.
   a. should
   b. shouldn't

3. The patient ____ eat salty and fatty foods.
   a. should
   b. shouldn't

4. The patient says, ____.
   a. "I understand."
   b. "I can't."

Conversation 2

5. The doctor is concerned about the patient's ____.
   a. lungs
   b. rings

6. The patient should stop ____.
   a. coughing
   b. smoking

7. The doctor thinks the patient should stop ____.
   a. right away
   b. next week

8. The patient says, "Thank you for the ____."
   a. right
   b. advice

C. The Right Choice

Circle the correct word.

1. I'm very concerned about your (floss (weight)).
2. You should do (a diet   sit-ups).
3. You should (daily   stop smoking) immediately.
4. I suggest that you (lose   quit) twenty pounds.
5. Thank you for the (suggest   advice).
6. You should stop eating fatty (foods   salty).
7. I'm concerned about your blood (style   pressure).
8. You should (stop   slow) down!
9. I (suggest   thank) that you take a vacation.
10. You should use dental floss (gums   daily).

D. Good Advice or Bad Advice?

Decide if each of the following is good advice or bad advice.

	Good Advice	Bad Advice
1. "You're a little heavy. You should go on a diet."	✔	
2. "I'm concerned about your lungs. You should do sit-ups."		
3. "You should eat salty foods every day. It's good for your back."		
4. "I'm concerned about your gums. You should use dental floss every day."		
5. "My doctor is concerned about my blood pressure. She thinks I should eat fatty foods."		
6. "I'm concerned about your life style. You should slow down and take a vacation."		

E. Open Road!

Complete the following about yourself.

1. How many hours do you sleep every night?

....

....

2. What do you do for exercise?

....

....

3. What healthy foods do you eat?

....

....

A. The Right Choice

Circle the correct word.

A. ((Here's) Where's)[1] your medicine.

B. Thank you.

A. Be sure to follow the (exit directions)[2] on the label.
(Take Make)[3] one tablet three times a day.

B. I understand. One tablet three times a (week day)[4].

A. That's (advice right)[5].

B. Crosswalk

teaspoon	=	tsp.	once a day	=	1×/day
capsule	=	cap.	twice a day	=	2×/day
tablet	=	tab.	three times a day	=	3×/day

ACROSS

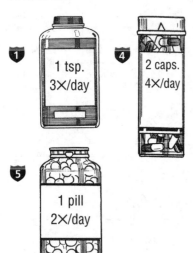

1. 1 tsp. 3×/day

4. 2 caps. 4×/day

5. 1 pill 2×/day

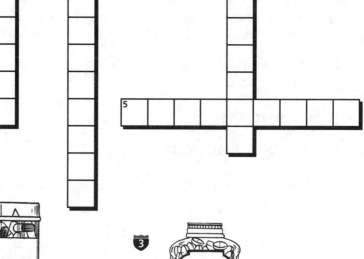

DOWN

1. 2 tsps. 1×/day

2. 2 caps. 2×/day

3. 1 tab. 4×/day

Report an Emergency

A. Listen

Listen to the conversations and answer the questions.

Conversation 1

1 a. The woman called 911.
   b. The woman called 411.

2 a. Her husband is bleeding.
   b. Her husband is choking.

3 a. Her last name is Mirror.
   b. Her last name is Miller.

4 a. The address is 15 Draper Avenue.
   b. The address is 50 Draper Avenue.

5 a. An emergency will come right away.
   b. An ambulance will come right away.

Conversation 2

6 a. The man is calling the Police Emergency Unit.
   b. The man is calling the emergency room.

7 a. There's a security guard in his apartment.
   b. There's a burglar in his apartment.

8 a. His first name is Richard.
   b. His last name is Richards.

9 a. His telephone number is 367-9805.
   b. His telephone number is 367-9905.

10 a. The ambulance will be there right away.
   b. The police will be there right away.

Conversation 3

11 a. Somebody is reporting an emergency to the Police Department.
   b. Somebody is reporting an emergency to the Fire Department.

12 a. The woman's house is on fire.
   b. The woman is having a heart attack.

13 a. The woman's last name is Martinez.
   b. The woman's last name is Sanchez.

14 a. The address is 40 Blake Street.
   b. The address is 40 Drake Street.

15 a. The Medical Department will be there right away.
   b. The Fire Department will be there right away.

Check-Up Test: Exits 4, 5, 6

A. Fill It In!

1 _____ married.
   a. I
   b. I do
   c. I'm   (c circled)

2 _____ you help me?
   a. Are
   b. Can
   c. Does

3 I _____ jewelry.
   a. sells
   b. sell
   c. salesperson

4 My husband and I _____ English.
   a. teachers
   b. teaching
   c. teach

5 What _____ your wife do?
   a. do
   b. does
   c. works

6 Richard _____ at the bakery.
   a. bake
   b. work
   c. works

7 _____ you speak Chinese?
   a. Can
   b. Does
   c. Is

8 I'm not a mechanic. I _____ fix cars.
   a. can
   b. doesn't
   c. can't

9 She's short _____ black hair.
   a. curly
   b. with
   c. straight

10 I'm looking for an _____.
   a. apartment
   b. capsule
   c. ear drops

11 _____ on the table.
   a. Looking
   b. Lies
   c. Sit

12 I take guitar lessons on _____.
   a. Tuesday
   b. after work
   c. it's Wednesday

13 Henry _____ a backache.
   a. does
   b. is
   c. has

14 I like your presentation. You're giving _____ very well.
   a. him
   b. it
   c. them

B. What's the Answer?

1 Am I training them all right?   Yes, _____ *you are* _____.

2 Can you assemble components?   Yes, _____.

3 Do you have a daughter?   No, _____.

4 Are they working today?   Yes, _____.

5 Is there an elevator in the building? No, _____.

C. What's the Word?

Complete the sentences.

1. _____Is_____ there a problem?

2. _____ you exercise?

3. _____ she dizzy?

4. _____ you allergic to this medicine?

5. _____ that include electricity?

6. _____ there any more eggs?

7. _____ he bleeding?

8. _____ there a history of heart disease in your family?

D. The 5th Wheel!

Which one doesn't belong?

1. apple   (beach)   tomato   bread

2. daughter   doctor   brother   mother

3. baseball   hockey   soccer   drama

4. aspirin   ear drops   gums   cough medicine

5. those   this   these   their

E. What's the Answer?

Answer the questions.

1. What's she looking for?

_____She's looking for rice._____

2. What do you do?

_____

3. What can she do?

_____

4. What's the matter with you?

_____

F. Listen

Listen and write the number you hear.

1. __9__ : _45_

2. _____ caps.

3. _____ Park Lane

4. Aisle _____

5. _____ bedrooms

6. $ _____ a month

Ask for Articles of Clothing in a Department Store

Student Text
Pages
112–113

A. The Right Choice

Circle the correct word.

A. Excuse me. Can **¹** me / **you** help **²** me / you ?

B. Certainly.

A. **³** I / I'm looking for a pair of **⁴** shoe / shoes .

B. **⁵** Shoe / Shoes are on that **⁶** rash / rack .

A. Thank you.

B. Listen

Listen and circle the word you hear.

1	dress	dresses	**7**	raincoats	raincoat
2	dress	dresses	**8**	pajama	pajamas
3	suit	suits	**9**	morning gown	evening gown
4	sweater	sweaters	**10**	pants	pant
5	hats	hat	**11**	rubbers	jackets
6	boots	suits	**12**	jersey	shirt

ACROSS

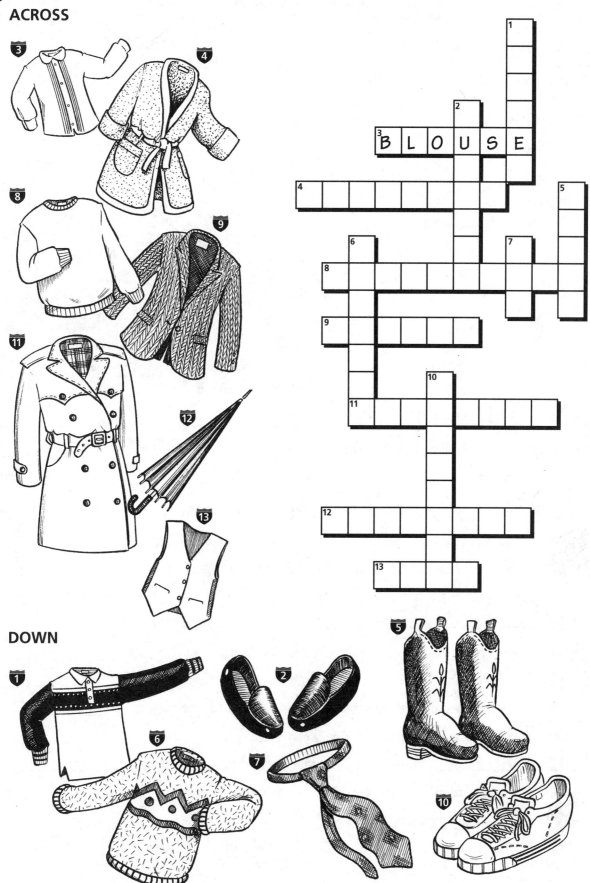

DOWN

Across clue 3 answer filled in: **BLOUSE**

A. Wrong Way!

Put the lines in the correct order.

___ Okay. Let's see . . . a small blue sweater. Here you are.

___ What size do you want?

___ Thank you very much.

_1_ May I help you?

___ Blue.

___ Yes, please. I'm looking for a sweater.

___ Small.

___ And what color?

B. Likely or Unlikely?

Are the following "likely" or "unlikely"?

		Likely	Unlikely
1	Bill is going to the park. He's wearing a pair of sneakers.	✔	
2	Monica is going to the mall. She's wearing orange pajamas.		
3	Susan is at school. She's wearing a yellow evening gown.		
4	I'm doing my homework. I'm wearing purple rubbers.		
5	My father is cleaning the garage. He's wearing a sweatshirt.		
6	The secretary in our office is wearing a pink bathrobe.		
7	Our supervisor, Mr. Peters, is wearing a red skirt today.		
8	The security guard is wearing an orange and gold jersey.		
9	The doctor is wearing a white jacket.		
10	It's cold today. I'm wearing a gray jacket and brown boots.		
11	The mechanic is fixing a car. She's wearing a white suit.		
12	Ms. Brooks is wearing her new blue suit to work today.		
13	I'm teaching an English class. I'm wearing a black raincoat.		

C. Open Road!

Tell about colors in your life.

1. My living room is ....
2. My bedroom is ....
3. My kitchen is ....
4. My favorite shoes are ....

5. My favorite jeans are ....
6. My favorite shirt is ....
7. My favorite sweater is ....
8. My favorite .... is ....

D. Wrong Way!

Change one letter to write an article of clothing.

1. racket   j a c k e t
2. roots   _ _ _ _ _
3. vast   _ _ _ _

4. boat   _ _ _ _ _
5. die   _ _ _
6. hit   _ _ _

E. WordRap: *Shopping*

Listen. Then clap and practice.

A. Where are the gloves?
B. I think they're on 2.
A. Where are you going?
B. I'm coming with you.

A. I'm looking for a jacket
And a pair of pants.
B. I'm looking for something
To wear to the dance.

A. Let's get a gift
For my sister Sue.
B. Let's get a gift
For my brother, too.

A. I want a sweater
Or a woolen vest.
B. My feet are tired.
I need to rest!

A. Which floor are we on?
B. I think we're on 3.
A. Where are the elevators?
B. Don't ask me!

A. Is there an escalator?
B. I don't know.
A. Where are the rest rooms?
I have to go!

A. What's the Word?

Complete the conversations.

large	long
short	tight
one	
pair	

1 A. How does the skirt fit?

B. It's too ___long___.

A. Do you want to try another ___one___?

B. Yes please.

2 A. How do the pants fit?

B. They're too _____.

A. Do you want to try on another _____?

B. Yes, please.

3 A. How do the gloves fit?

B. They're too _____.

A. Do you want to try another _____?

B. Yes, please.

4 A. How does the suit fit?

B. It's too _____.

A. Do you want to try on another _____?

B. Yes, please.

B. Listen

Listen and choose the correct answer.

1
a. The blouse fits.
b. The blouse doesn't fit.

2
a. The pants fit.
b. The pants don't fit.

3
a. The boots are too tight.
b. The suit is too tight.

4
a. The woman is trying on a shirt.
b. The woman is trying on a skirt.

5
a. The socks fit.
b. The socks don't fit.

6
a. The sneakers are too big.
b. The sneakers are too small.

A. The Right Choice

Circle the correct word.

1. Excuse me. Where (is **are**) VCRs?
2. TVs are (on   in) the back of the store.
3. Bedroom furniture is (on   in) the third floor.
4. You can find sofas on the (seven   second) floor.
5. The restaurant is (near   in) the elevator.
6. Excuse me. (Where are   Where is) the dressing room?
7. Radios are (in   on) the basement.

B. Number Match

Match the numbers.

_c_	1	eighth	a. 6th	___	6	fourth	f. 9th
___	2	third	b. 3rd	___	7	first	g. 7th
___	3	tenth	c. 8th	___	8	ninth	h. 4th
___	4	second	d. 10th	___	9	fifth	i. 1st
___	5	sixth	e. 2nd	___	10	seventh	j. 5th

C. Wrong Way!

Put the words in the correct order.

A. Men's   me.   the   Excuse   Where's   Department?

_____Excuse me._____

B. store.   the   the   It's   of   in   back

_____

A. is   And   restaurant?   where   the

_____

B. floor.   on   seventh   It's   the

_____

81

A. What's the Line?

Complete the conversations.

> Excuse me, but I think they're on sale this week.
>
> Oh. You're right. It's half price. I'm sorry.
>
> With the tax, that comes to $27.51.
>
> I'd like to buy this camera.
>
> Oh. You're right. They're twenty percent off. I apologize.
>
> With the tax, that comes to $15.74.

1 A. ___I'd like to buy this camera___.

B. Okay. That's $29.99.

A. Excuse me, but I don't think that's right price. I think this camera is on sale this week.

B. _____

_____

A. That's okay.

B. _____

_____

2 A. I'd like to buy these boots.

B. Okay. That's $32.75

A. _____

_____

B. _____

_____

A. That's okay.

B. _____

_____

B. Listen

Listen and circle the amount of money you hear.

1 ($34.50) $43.50   **4** $455.50 $415.50   **7** $17.00 $70.00

2 $315.99 $305.99   **5** $50.17 $17.50   **8** $245.50 $255.50

3 $14.00 $40.00   **6** $77.98 $67.98   **9** $122.20 $102.20

C. Matching

Match the items and the departments.

_e_ **1** skirts

___ **2** ties

___ **3** children's jackets

___ **4** sneakers

___ **5** TVs

___ **6** refrigerators

___ **7** earrings

___ **8** Swiss chocolate

___ **9** sofa

DIRECTORY

a. **Jewelry Department**

b. **Home Entertainment Department**

c. **Gourmet Food Department**

d. **Men's Clothing Department**

e. **Women's Clothing Department**

f. **Children's Department**

g. **Furniture Department**

h. **Shoe Department**

i. **Appliance Department**

D. What's the Line?

Complete the conversation.

Do you want to buy a second item? And the color? May I help you?
What size do you want? Your address, please?

A. J. J. Rean Company. ____May I help you____?¹

B. Yes. I'd like to buy the woman's shirt on page 72 of the catalog.

A. _____?²

B. Medium.

A. _____?³

B. Yellow.

A. _____?⁴

B. No, I don't.

A. _____?⁵

B. 133 Baker Avenue, Chester, New York 10918.

A. That comes to $29.99 with shipping. You should have your shirt on Tuesday.

Return Items to a Department Store

Student Text
Pages
124–125

A. The Right Choice

Circle the correct word.

1 This textbook is too (small (easy)).

2 This purse is too (large   short).

3 This coat is too (difficult   heavy).

4 These jeans are too (quiet   tight).

5 This video game is too (easy   heavy).

6 These pajamas are too (noisy   large).

B. What's the Response?

Choose the correct response.

1 What's the matter with this purse?
   a. They're too small.
   (b.) It's too small.

2 Do you have the receipt?
   a. I'd like a refund, please.
   b. Yes. Here you are.

3 I'd like to buy these videogames.
   a. Okay. That's $35.99.
   b. Do you have a receipt?

4 How do the gloves fit?
   a. They're white.
   b. They're tight.

5 Do you want to exchange it?
   a. It's too noisy.
   b. No. I'd like a refund, please.

6 I'd like to return this workbook.
   a. Okay. That's $12.00.
   b. What's the matter with it?

7 Where are the typewriters?
   a. It's on the fourth floor.
   b. They're on the fourth floor.

8 What size do you want?
   a. Large.
   b. Heavy.

C. Listen

Listen and choose the correct answer.

Conversation 1

1 She wants to return a _____.
   (a.) shirt
   b. skirt

2 It's too _____.
   a. short
   b. tight

3 She _____ the receipt.
   a. has
   b. doesn't have

Conversation 2

4 He wants to return a _____.
   a. raincoat
   b. bathrobe

5 It's too _____.
   a. heavy
   b. easy

6 He _____ the receipt.
   a. has
   b. doesn't have

Use the Services of a Post Office

Student Text Pages 126–127

A. The Right Choice

Circle the correct word

1. I want to (mail (buy)) some stamps, please.

2. I want to mail a (package   money order), please.

3. I want to (send   buy) a registered letter, please.

4. I want to (mail   file) a change of address form.

5. I want to buy (an aerogramme   a package), please.

6. I want to buy (money order   stamps), please.

B. Crosswalk

change of address form	money order	send	Number
aerogramme	stamps	mail	buy

ACROSS

2. I'd like to buy some _____.

4. Where can I buy an _____?

6. I want to _____ a money order.

7. I'd like to _____ this package to France.

8. You can buy a money order at Window _____ 3.

DOWN

1. Can I file a _____, please?

3. You can _____ a package at the window on the left.

5. I want to buy a _____ to pay my rent.

2. S T A M P S

A. Listen

Listen to the conversation and answer the questions.

1. (a.) The conversation is at the post office.
   b. The conversation is at the bank.

2. a. The woman wants to mail some letters.
   b. The woman wants to mail some packages.

3. a. She wants to send them to San Juan.
   b. She wants to send them to Hong Kong.

4. a. She wants to send them third class.
   b. She wants to sent them first class.

5. a. She's sending English textbooks
      and videogames.
   b. She's sending French textbooks
      and videogames.

6. a. She wants to insure them for $6.00.
   b. She wants to insure them for $60.00.

7. a. The total is seven dollars and thirteen cents.
   b. The total is thirteen dollars and seven cents.

B. The 5th Wheel!

Which one doesn't belong?

1 aerogramme	registered letter	package	(change of address form)
2 insure	third class	second class	first class
3 black	green	short	yellow
4 small	noisy	large	tight
5 earrings	coat	dress	shirt
6 radio	TV	VCR	textbook
7 basement	elevator	seventh floor	second floor
8 in the back of	near	in the front of	window
9 fourth	eleven	eighth	tenth
10 gloves	rubbers	sneakers	boots
11 has	does	are	is

Tell About Weekend Plans

Student Text Pages 132–133

A. The Right Choice

Circle the correct words.

A. What are you | (going to do)¹ / go to do | this weekend?

B. I'm | going² / going to | see a play. How about you?

A. I'm going | to stay home³ / stay home | and write letters.

B. Well, have a good | stay home⁴ / weekend | !

A. You, too.

B. Listen

Listen and circle the sentence you hear.

1. a. I'm going to clean my apartment.   (b.) I'm going to clean my garage.

2. a. They're going to do their homework.   b. They're going to go to work.

3. a. He's going to study at home.   b. He's going to relax at home.

4. a. He's going to visit his grandchildren.   b. She's going to visit her grandchildren.

5. a. I'm going to visit my grandmother.   b. I'm going to visit my grandchildren.

6. a. They're going to study English.   b. We're going to study English.

7. a. She's going to take her children to the zoo.   b. She's going to take her children to the park.

C. Matching Lines

Match the questions and answers.

_b_ **1** What are you and Charles going to do tonight?

a. I'm going to move to Japan and study Japanese.

___ **2** What are you going to do tonight?

b. We're going to go to a movie.

___ **3** What exciting things are going to happen in your life this year?

c. I'm going to watch my favorite TV program.

___ **4** What are you going to do when you finish school?

d. He's probably going to go to graduate school.

___ **5** What's your son going to do next year?

e. I think she's going to stay home and read.

___ **6** What's your wife going to do this Sunday?

f. We're going to look for jobs.

___ **7** What are many people going to do this year?

g. He's going to take a vacation and visit his grandchildren.

___ **8** What's your grandfather going to do next year?

h. I'm going to take another one. How about you?

___ **9** What are you going to do when you finish this course?

i. They're going to stop smoking and stop eating fatty foods.

D. Open Road!

Interview two classmates. Ask them: "What are you going to do this year?" Write their answers.

....

....

....

....

....

....

....

....

....

....

Make Plans for the Day

A. Wrong Way!

Put the lines in the correct order.

___ It's cloudy. Do you want to go to a museum?

_1_ What do you want to do today?

___ Sure. That's a good idea.

___ I don't know. What's the weather like?

B. What's the Line?

Complete the conversations.

| have a picnic | stay home | take umbrellas |
| see a movie | go skiing | go swimming |

1

A. What's the weather like?

B. It's cloudy.

A. Do you want to _____

_____see a movie_____?

A. What's the weather like?

B. It's sunny.

A. Do you want to _____

_____?

3

A. What's the weather like?

B. It's hot.

A. Do you want to _____

_____?

4

A. What's the weather like?

B. It's raining.

A. Do you want to _____

_____?

5

A. What's the weather like?

B. It's snowing.

A. Do you want to _____

_____?

6

A. What's the weather like?

B. It's cold.

A. Do you want to _____

_____?

89

C. Crosswalk

ACROSS

2 

3 

6 

7 

2 SUNNY

DOWN

1 

2 

4 

5 

D. What's the Word?

Complete the sentences.

want to	wants to

1. It's cold, and my grandmother wants to stay at home and watch TV.
2. I ____________ fix my car and have a picnic at the zoo.
3. My children ____________ see a movie.
4. My brother ____________ take the bus downtown and go to the mall.
5. It's sunny, and we ____________ go to the park.
6. My sister ____________ go skating today.
7. What about you? What do you ____________ do?

E. Listen

Listen to the temperatures in Fahrenheit and Centigrade. Write the numbers you hear.

Beijing: _50_ ° F   _10_ ° C

Paris: ____ ° F   ____ ° C

New York: ____ ° F   ____ ° C

Caracas: ____ ° F   ____ ° C

Manila: ____ ° F   ____ ° C

Chicago: ____ ° F   ____ ° C

Anchorage: ____ ° F   ____ ° C

San Francisco: ____ ° F   ____ ° C

F. The Right Choice

Complete the following.

1 I want to go swimming today.
   a. It's cold.
   (b.) It's hot.

2 I'd like to go skating.
   a. It's cold.
   b. It's hot and humid.

3 We should go to a museum.
   a. It's sunny.
   b. It's cloudy.

4 You should take your umbrella to work.
   a. It's raining.
   b. It's hazy.

5 I'd like to go on a picnic today.
   a. It's cold and snowing.
   b. It's sunny.

6 My children want to go skiing.
   a. It's snowing.
   b. It's raining.

G. Open Road!

Ask five classmates about the weather in their country.

What's the weather like in your country?

Name	Country	Weather

A. The Right Choice

Circle the correct word.

A. Do you want to go dancing Saturday night?

B. Saturday night? I'm afraid I (can (can't))¹. I (have to   has to)² work.

A. That's too (glad   bad)³.

B. Maybe we (can   can't)⁴ go dancing another time.

B. What's the Word?

Complete the conversation.

> have to   has to

A. I'm moving to a new apartment this Saturday. Can you possibly help me move some furniture?

B. I'm afraid I can't. I ___have to___¹ go to the dentist. How about your brother?

A. He can't help me. He _____² go to the airport with our grandmother.

B. How about Bob and Maria?

A. They can't help me either. They _____³ work this Saturday.

B. That's too bad. How about Jose?

A. Jose _____⁴ take his children to the zoo.

C. Polite or Not Polite?

Choose the polite response.

1. Do you want to go skating on Sunday?
   a. No.
   (b.) I'm afraid I can't.

2. Can you and your husband come to my party next weekend?
   a. I'm sorry. We can't. We have to work.
   b. No. We don't like parties.

3. Do you want to come to dinner on Friday?
   a. I don't want to.
   b. I'm afraid I can't. I have to study.

4. Do your children want to go to the park with my children this afternoon?
   a. I'm afraid they can't. They have to go to the dentist.
   b. They don't like your children.

A. Wrong Way!

Put the lines in the correct order.

___ Yes, I did.

___ I baked some cookies.

_1_ Did you have a good weekend?

___ What did you do?

B. What's the Word?

Complete the conversations.

| did   didn't | watch   paint   go   fix   drive   play |

1 A. Did Janet fix her bicycle last week?

B. No, she __didn't__. She __fixed__ her car.

2 A. Did the Chens paint their kitchen this week?

B. Yes, they _____.

3 A. Did you watch a comedy on TV last night?

B. No, we _____. We _____ an adventure movie.

4 A. Did Jim drive to the beach today?

B. No, he _____. He _____ to the shopping mall.

5 A. Did Mrs. Lee play the piano for her guests?

B. No, she _____. She _____ her violin.

6 A. Did your sisters go to the museum on Saturday?

B. Yes, they _____.

C. The 5th Wheel!

Which one sounds different?

1 cooked	(rested)	washed	fixed
2 cleaned	played	listened	baked
3 watched	planted	rested	painted
4 raincoats	shoes	socks	pants
5 played	watched	baked	relaxed
6 ties	shoes	sweaters	pants
7 blouses	offices	socks	dresses
8 earrings	gloves	stamps	jeans

D. What's the Response?

Choose the correct response.

1 Did you play golf yesterday?
   a. No, I did.
   (b.) No, I didn't.

2 I wrote letters to my friends.
   a. What are you writing about?
   b. What did you write about?

3 Did you have a good weekend?
   a. Yes, I did. I played tennis.
   b. Yes, I play tennis.

4 What did you bake?
   a. I bake cookies.
   b. I baked cookies.

5 I didn't study English last night.
   a. What did you do?
   b. What do you do?

6 I read five magazines yesterday.
   a. What magazines did you read?
   b. What magazines do you read?

7 What did you do last weekend?
   a. I relax every weekend.
   b. I relaxed at home.

8 Did you go sailing?
   a. No, I don't.
   b. No, I didn't.

E. Open Road!

What did you do last week?

....

....

....

....

A. Listen

Listen to the conversations and answer the questions.

Conversation 1

1 a. This woman wants to go skiing today.
      (b.) This woman doesn't want to go skiing today.

2 a. They went skiing last weekend.
      b. They went skiing last night.

3 a. She wants to go skating today.
      b. She went skating last weekend.

Conversation 2

4 a. These people want to do something outdoors today.
      b. These people want to do something indoors today.

5 a. They're going sailing today.
      b. They went sailing yesterday.

6 a. They're going to go sailing today.
      b. They're going to go swimming today.

B. Crosswalk

Write the past tense for each verb.

ACROSS

1 go

2 take

3 drive

5 have

DOWN

1 write

4 read

A. The Right Choice

Circle the correct word

A. ((Where)   What)¹ were you yesterday evening?
I called you, but you (weren't   wasn't)² home.

B. That's right. I (weren't   wasn't)³. I was at a concert.

A. Oh. (What   Who)⁴ did you (see   hear)⁵?

B. I (heard   hear)⁶ the Philadelphia Orchestra.

A. (Do   Did)⁷ you enjoy it?

B. Yes. It was excellent.

B. Matching Lines

Match the questions and answers.

_d_ **1** Were you home last Sunday afternoon?   a. They were at the baseball stadium.

___ **2** Where were you?   b. Our dog was at home on Sunday.

___ **3** How was the food?   c. No, it wasn't. It was cloudy.

___ **4** Was your husband at the restaurant?   d. No, I wasn't.

___ **5** Where were your children?   e. It was exciting.

___ **6** What game did they see?   f. I was at a Greek restaurant.

___ **7** How was the game?   g. He was outdoors on the patio.

___ **8** Was the weather good?   h. The White Sox against the Red Sox.

___ **9** Who was at home on Sunday?   i. It was delicious.

___ **10** Where was your dog?   j. Yes, he was.

C. What's the Response?

Choose the correct response.

1 Were you home yesterday morning?
  a. No, I wasn't.
  b. I'm going home tonight.

2 Did you enjoy it?
  a. It was raining.
  b. Yes. It was excellent.

3 Who did you hear?
  a. The baseball game.
  b. The Philadelphia Orchestra.

4 Do you recommend the movie?
  a. Yes, I do.
  b. Yes, I am.

5 How was the service?
  a. It was delicious.
  b. It was excellent.

6 When did you go?
  a. Last weekend.
  b. Tomorrow.

7 What did you play?
  a. At the theater.
  b. I played golf.

8 Who did you go with?
  a. I went with my grandmother.
  b. I went to the mall.

9 What did you have at the restaurant?
  a. I had moussaka.
  b. I had a sore throat.

10 What play did you see?
  a. I played tennis.
  b. "The Friendly Garden."

11 Where were you and your family last week?
  a. We were in San Diego.
  b. No, we weren't.

12 How was the party last night?
  a. It was at Bill's house.
  b. It was terrible. The music was awful.

13 What game did you see?
  a. The baseball stadium.
  b. The Yankees against the Dodgers.

14 I called you, but you weren't home.
  a. I was at the movies.
  b. That's right. I was home.

D. WordRap: *How Was Your Weekend?*

Listen. Then clap and practice.

A. How was your weekend?
   What did you do?
B. I got up early and went to the zoo.

A. How was your vacation?
   Where did you go?
B. I took a plane to Mexico.

A. How was the party?
   Did you have a lot of fun?
B. I talked and danced with everyone.

A. How was the exam?
   Did you do okay?
B. I knew all the answers,
   And I got an A!

A. Listen

Listen to the conversation and answer yes or no.

1	She likes to play golf.	(Yes)	No
2	He likes to do yoga.	Yes	No
3	He went jogging today.	Yes	No
4	He went jogging before work.	Yes	No
5	She played golf this morning.	Yes	No

B. What's the Word?

Complete the sentences.

like to	likes to

go	walk	drive
wash	read	write

1 Peter _____likes to go_____ to
science fiction movies.

2 We _____
to the mountains.

3 Mr. and Mrs. Perez _____
in the park on Sunday afternoons.

4 Tina _____
her car every weekend.

5 The Smiths _____
biographies.

6 Arnold _____
letters to his friends.

A. Fill It In!

Fill in the correct answer.

1 I _____ work late.
   a. has to
   b. having to
   c. have to *(circled)*

2 _____ cold today.
   a. We
   b. It's
   c. It

3 Nancy _____ to read novels.
   a. likes
   b. like
   c. want

4 _____ this letter going?
   a. How
   b. Does
   c. Where's

5 I'd like to buy _____ sneakers.
   a. them
   b. those
   c. that

6 We went there _____.
   a. tomorrow
   b. yesterday
   c. tonight

7 Do you want to play tennis _____?
   a. yesterday evening
   b. tonight
   c. last night

8 _____ you have a good weekend?
   a. Does
   b. Do
   c. Did

9 We _____ a walk in the park yesterday.
   a. took
   b. drove
   c. take

10 Where _____ you last night?
   a. was
   b. did
   c. were

11 I _____ swim for exercise.
   a. like
   b. like to do
   c. like to

12 Maybe we _____ see a play this weekend.
   a. did
   b. can
   c. going to

B. What's the Word?

Complete the sentences.

1 There pajamas are _too_ tight.

2 We _____ jogging yesterday.

3 I'm looking _____ a new dress.

4 I'd _____ to buy this color TV.

5 I'm afraid I _____ go to the movies.

6 I have _____ study tonight.

7 How _____ this jacket fit?

8 What's the matter _____ it?

9 It's going to _____ cloudy tomorrow.

10 What movie _____ you see yesterday?

11 I called you, but you _____ home.

12 _____ raining today.

13 It's in the back _____ the store.

14 Did you have _____ good weekend?

C. The Right Choice

Circle the correct WH-word.

1. (Where's (What's)) the matter with it?
2. (When   Who) is the meeting?
3. (Where   What) were you last night?
4. (When   What) are you going to do?
5. (Where   What) is this package going?

6. (How   What) do you want to do?
7. (How   Which) do these boots fit?
8. (Where   When) are the stamps?
9. (How   What) size do you want?
10. (Who   How) do you want to send it?

D. The 5th Wheel!

Which one doesn't belong?

1. humid   sunny   (swim)   cloudy
2. jacket   camera   shirt   blouse
3. long   black   gray   white
4. boots   shoes   belts   sneakers
5. rack   table   coat   counter
6. money order   window   package   letter
7. went   wrote   rested   bake
8. extra-large   small   tight   medium
9. blouses   pants   socks   raincoats

E. Listen

Listen and choose the correct response.

1. a. Thank you very much.
   b.) It's in the basement.

2. a. Yes, it is.
   b. First class.

3. a. Certainly.
   b. You're welcome.

4. a. She's going to go to a concert.
   b. A red sweater and black pants.

5. a. Okay. That's seventy-nine fifty.
   b. It's in the front of the store.

6. a. What size do you want?
   b. Do you have the receipt?

7. a. I'm going to the library.
   b. They're too difficult.

8. a. It's hot and humid.
   b. Let's go to the museum.

9. a. Yes. I played golf.
   b. I'm going to go out for dinner.

10. a. I swam this morning.
    b. I like to do yoga.

11. a. That's too bad.
    b. That sounds like fun.

12. a. I write letters.
    b. I wrote letters.

100

SCRIPTS FOR LISTENING EXERCISES

Listen and circle the word you hear.

1. A. Hi. How are you?
   B. Fine. And you?
   A. Fine, thanks. I'd like to introduce you to my husband, Michael.
2. A. Hi. I'd like to introduce you to my mother, Mrs. Smith.
   B. Nice to meet you.
3. A. Hi. How are you?
   B. Fine, thanks. And you?
   A. Fine, thanks. I'd like to introduce you to my sister, Barbara.
4. A. I'd like to introduce you to my wife, Susan.
   B. Nice to meet you.
5. A. This is my brother, Eric.
   B. Nice to meet you.
   C. Nice meeting you, too.
6. A. Hi, Bob. How are you?
   B. Fine. And you?
   A. Fine, thanks. I'd like to introduce you to my father.
7. A. Hi, Maria. How are you?
   B. Fine, thanks. And you?
   A. Fine. I'd like to introduce you to my husband.
8. A. Hi, Sally. How are you?
   B. Fine, thanks. And you?
   A. Fine, thanks. I'd like to introduce you to my mother.

Page 3

Listen and circle the correct name.

1. A. What's your last name?
   B. Dillon.
   A. Could you spell that, please?
   B. D-I-L-L-O-N.
2. A. And your last name?
   B. It's Ramos. R-A-M-O-S.
3. A. Hello. How are you?
   B. Fine. And you?
   A. Fine, thank you. What's your last name, please?
   B. Barnes. B-A-R-N-E-S.
4. A. And your last name, please?
   B. Vassil. V-A-S-S-I-L.
5. A. What's your name?
   B. Alan Beatty.
   A. Could you spell that, please?
   B. B-E-A-T-T-Y.
6. A. What's your name?
   B. Mr. Mazer.
   A. Could you spell that, please?
   B. M-A-Z-E-R.
7. A. And your name?
   B. Barry Lynch.
   A. Could you spell that, please?
   B. L-Y-N-C-H.
8. A. My name is Margaret Kling.
   B. Nice to meet you. Could you

spell your last name, please?
   A. K-L-I-N-G.
9. A. And your name?
   B. Mrs. Wicks.
   A. Could you spell that, please?
   B. W-I-C-K-S.
10. A. My name is Frieda Cramer.
   B. Could you spell your last name, please?
   A. Sure. C-R-A-M-E-R.

Page 5

Listen and put a check next to the correct answer.

1. A. Hello, Mr. Miller. What's your address, please?
   B. 17 Baker Street.
2. A. And your telephone number?
   B. 463-9027.
3. A. Nice meeting you, Mr. Miller.
4. A. Hello, Mrs. Ramirez. What's your telephone number, please?
   B. 531-7021.
5. A. And your address?
   B. 13 Draper Avenue.
6. A. 13 Draper Avenue?
7. A. Hello, Mrs. Jordan. What's your address, please?
   B. 3 Pond Road.
8. A. Could you spell that?
   B. P-O-N-D.
9. A. And your telephone number?
   B. 891-4362.

Page 6

Listen and choose the correct answer.

1. Hi. What's your name?
2. Where are you from?
3. Oh. Are you from Toronto?
4. I'd like to introduce my wife, Barbara.
5. Where are you from, Barbara?
6. Are you from London?
7. Are you Kenji?
8. What's your last name?
9. Are you from Osaka?
10. Hello. My name is David.
11. Where are you from?
12. Are you from Los Angeles?

Page 10

Listen and fill out the form.

A. Hello. I'm Mr. Chang. Welcome to the ExpressWays English School. What's your first name?
B. My first name is Carlos.
A. And your last name?
B. Reyes.
A. Could you spell that, please?
B. R-E-Y-E-S.
A. What's your address?

B. 17 Porter Street.
A. Could you spell that too, please?
B. P-O-R-T-E-R.
A. And your telephone number?
B. 459-3217.
A. And where are you from, Mr. Reyes?
B. Puerto Rico.
A. Oh. Are you from San Juan?
B. No. I'm from Ponce.
A. Ponce?
B. Yes. Ponce. P-O-N-C-E.

Page 14

Listen and choose the correct answer.

1. My name is Keiko Asamura. I'm not from Osaka. I'm from Tokyo.
2. I'd like to introduce Brian and Kate Wild. They aren't American. They're Canadian.
3. A. Is this 742-1980?
   B. No, it isn't. You have the wrong number.
   A. Sorry.
4. A. Are you Marco?
   B. No, I'm not. I'm Pablo.
5. A. Am I on Third Avenue?
   B. No, you aren't. You're on Myrtle Avenue.
6. A. Are you Maria and Franco?
   B. No, we aren't. Maria and Franco are our mother and father.

Page 16

Listen and circle the place you hear.

1. A. Hello. This is Julie. Is John there?
   B. No, he isn't. He's at the supermarket.
   A. Oh, I see. I'll call back later. Thank you.
2. A. Hello. This is Sylvia. Is Janet there?
   B. No, she isn't. She's at the bank.
   A. Oh, I see. I'll call back later. Thank you.
3. A. Hello. Are Mr. and Mrs. Green there?
   B. No, they aren't. They're at the library.
   A. Oh, I see. I'll call back later. Thank you.
4. A. Hello. This is Jim. How are you?
   B. Fine. And you?
   A. Fine, thanks. Are Bill and Bob there?
   B. No, they aren't. They're at the laundromat.
   A. Oh, I see. I'll call back later. Thank you.
5. A. Hi. This is Susie. Is Jenny there?
   B. No, she isn't. She's at school.

A. Oh, I see. I'll call back later. Thank you.
6. A. Hello. This is Hector. Is Jose there?
   B. No, he isn't. He's at the park.
   A. Oh, I see. I'll call back later. Thank you.

Page 19

Listen and choose the correct answer.

1. I'm not fixing my bicycle. I'm fixing my car.
2. Dan isn't doing his exercises. He's doing his homework.
3. She isn't washing the dishes. She's walking the dog.
4. I'm looking for my contact lens.
5. The dog isn't eating dinner. It's eating lunch.
6. My sister and I are brushing our teeth.
7. I'm combing my hair.
8. They aren't cleaning their apartment. They're cleaning their garage.

Page 20

Listen and check the activities you hear.

1. A. Hello, Miguel? This is Frank.
   B. Hi. How are you doing?
   A. Pretty good. Listen, what are you doing?
   B. I'm fixing my car. How about you?
   A. I'm eating dinner and feeding the baby.
2. A. Hi, Jenny and Tommy. What are you doing?
   B. I'm washing the dishes, and Tommy is brushing his teeth. How about you?
   A. I'm studying.
3. A. Hi. How are you?
   B. Fine. And you?
   A. Fine, thanks. Where are you going?
   B. I'm going to school, and Steve is going to the movies. How about you? Where are you going?
   A. I'm going to the zoo.
4. A. Hi, Kenji. How are you?
   B. Fine. And you?
   A. Fine, thanks. I'd like to introduce my parents, Mr. and Mrs. Sanchez. They're going to the post office, and I'm going to the supermarket. How about you?
   B. I'm going to the airport. I'm going to Miami.

Page 25

Listen and circle the letter for each place.

1. The hotel is on Prescott Avenue, next to the mall.
2. There's a hospital on Center Street, across from the post office.
3. The drug store is on Front Street, around the corner from the supermarket.
4. There's a school on Front Street, around the corner from the clinic.
5. There's a fire station on North Avenue, between the bank and the supermarket.
6. The parking lot is across from the bus station.
7. The gas station is next to the post office.

Page 26

Listen and choose the correct answer.

1. A. Excuse me. Does this train go to Toronto?
   B. No, it doesn't. It goes to Denver.
2. A. Tell me, which bus goes downtown?
   B. The Number 60 bus.
3. A. Does this bus go to New York?
   B. No, it doesn't. It goes to Yorktown.
4. A. Excuse me. Does this plane go to Peru?
   B. Yes, it does.
5. A. Excuse me. Which train goes to the airport?
   B. The Number 30 train.
6. A. Tell me, does this ship go to Panama?
   B. Yes, it does. First it goes to Colombia, and then it goes to Panama.
7. A. Does this bus go to Oak Street?
   B. No, it doesn't. The Number 63 bus goes to Oak Street.
8. A. Excuse me. Does this plane go to San Diego?
   B. Yes, it does. First it goes to San Francisco, and then it goes to San Diego.
9. A. Tell me, does this plane go to Rome?
   B. No, it doesn't. It goes to Nome.
10. A. Which bus goes to the clinic?
    B. The Number 22 bus.

Page 28

Listen and complete the bus schedule.

A. Riverdale Bus Company.
B. Hello. Tell me, which bus goes to the airport?
A. Bus Number 64. It goes from the Park Street bus station to the airport. First, it stops downtown at the mall. Then it stops at the train station. And then it stops at the airport.
B. Thank you very much.

A. Riverdale Bus Company.
B. Hello. Tell me, does Bus Number 64 go to the hospital?
A. No, it doesn't, but Bus Number 16 does. It goes to the hospital from downtown. First it stops at the park. Then it stops at the zoo. Then it stops at the library. And then it stops at the hospital.
B. Thank you.

A. Riverdale Bus Company.
B. Hello. Tell me, is there a Number 54 bus?
A. Yes, there is. It goes from the airport to the hotel. Then it stops at the museum. And then it stops at the theater.
B. Thank you very much.

Page 29

Look at the map and listen to the directions. If the directions are correct, write **C**. If they are incorrect, write **I**.

1. A. Excuse me. Can you tell me how to get to the library?
   B. Yes. Walk THAT way. The library is on the left, next to the movie theater.
   A. Thank you.
2. A. Excuse me. Where's the bank?
   B. It's on the right, next to the fire station.
   A. Thank you.
3. A. Excuse me. How do I get to the hospital?
   B. Walk THAT way. The hospital is on the right, between the library and the clinic.
   A. Thank you.
4. A. Excuse me. Can you tell me how to get to the park?
   B. Yes. Walk THAT way. The park is on the left, across from the fire station.
   A. Thanks.
5. A. Excuse me. How do I get to the police station?
   B. Walk THAT way. The police station is on the right, next to the bus station.
   A. Thank you.
6. A. Excuse me. Is there a movie theater nearby?
   B. Yes. Walk THAT way. The movie theater is on the right, between the fire station and the library.
   A. Thank you.

Page 32

Listen and label the correct places.

1. A. Excuse me. I'm lost! Can you possibly tell me how to get to the Seaside Mall?
   B. Sure. Take the Northgate Expressway and get off at Exit 34. Turn left on Third Avenue and look for the mall on the left, across from the bank. Have you got that?
   A. I understand. Thank you very much.
2. A. Excuse me. Can you tell me how to get to the Seaview Zoo?

B. Sure. Take the Second Avenue bus and get off at the bank.
A. I'm sorry. WHERE do I get off?
B. At the bank. The Seaview Zoo is across from the bank.
A. Thanks very much.

3. A. Excuse me. I'm lost! How do I get to Ocean Park?
B. Drive THAT way three miles. Then take the Seaside Expressway and get off at Exit 45.
A. Okay.
B. Then turn right on First Avenue and look for Ocean Park on the right, across from Wet Water Park. Have you got that?
A. Yes. Thank you.

4. A. Excuse me. Is there a drug store nearby?
B. Yes, there is. There's a drug store on Second Avenue. Walk THAT way to Second Avenue. Go two blocks and look for the Seaview Drug Store on the right, across from Wet Water Park. Have you got that?
A. Yes. I understand. Thank you very much.

5. A. Excuse me. I'm lost. Can you tell me how to get to the Oceanside Hotel?
B. Sure. Take the Seaside Expressway and get off at Exit 42. Okay so far?
A. Yes. I'm following you.
B. Turn right on First Avenue and look for the hotel on the right, across from the Ocean Beach Cinema. Have you got that?
A. Yes. Thank you.

Page 35

Listen and write the number you hear.

1. Is this Bus Number 56?
2. Get off at Exit 23.
3. Take the expressway and get off at Exit 68.
4. Drive THAT way ten blocks.
5. My address is sixty-two eighteen Riverside Drive.
6. The number is 547-2155.
7. Mr. Chen's address is forty-six nineteen Central Avenue.
8. Is this 965-3280?

Page 39

Listen and circle the correct answer.

1. A. Is the rent $475 a month?
B. No. It's $485.
2. A. Does the rent include utilities?
B. It includes everything except the parking fee.
3. A. How much is the parking?
B. It's $34 a month.
4. A. Do you want to see the apartment?
B. Yes, I think so.

Page 42

Listen and circle the word you hear.

1. Where do you want these rugs?
2. How about these chairs?
3. How do you spell that name?
4. Are there waterbeds in those bedrooms?
5. Where do you want this crib?
6. Do you want to see these closets?
7. Put that picture in the bedroom.
8. Have you got that?

Page 45

Listen and circle the word you hear.

1. A. What are you looking for?
B. Lettuce.
A. Sorry. There isn't any lettuce. I'll get some more when I go to the supermarket.
2. A. Is there any cheese?
B. Sorry. There isn't.
3. A. I'm afraid there aren't any more eggs.
B. There aren't?
4. A. Is there any milk in the refrigerator?
B. No. Sorry. There isn't.
5. A. There aren't any more bananas.
B. There aren't?
6. A. Is there any ice cream in the refrigerator?
B. Yes, there is.
7. A. Are there any apples left?
B. No, there aren't.
8. A. I'm looking for an orange.
B. Sorry. There aren't any oranges in the house.
9. A. Are there any cookies left?
B. Sorry. There aren't.

Page 46

Listen to the conversations and complete the missing information.

1. A. Excuse me. Where are the potatoes?
B. They're in Aisle 3.
A. I'm sorry. Did you say "T"?
B. No. "3."
A. Oh. Thank you.
2. A. Excuse me. Where's the yogurt?
B. It's in Aisle 8.
A. I'm sorry. Did you say "A"?
B. No. "8."
A. Oh. Thank you.

Page 51

What can Linda do? Listen and circle "can" or "can't."

My name is Linda Chang. I can play the violin, but I can't play the piano. I can dance and I can sing, but I can't write novels. I can fix a radio, but I can't fix a car. I can't speak Italian, but I'm sure I can learn quickly. I can speak French. I can teach French, too. I'm an experienced teacher. And . . . oh, yes. I can use a computer, but I can't design a computer.

Page 52

Listen and write the number under the correct person.

1. A. Please give this to Ms. Long in Shipping.
B. I'm sorry, but I'm new here. What does she look like?
A. She's average height, with curly gray hair.
2. A. Please give this to Mr. Hurley in the Personnel Office.
B. I'm sorry, but I'm new here. What does he look like?
A. He's heavy, with straight black hair.
3. A. Please give this to Millie Hastings in the mailroom.
B. I'm sorry, but I'm new here. What does she look like?
A. She's tall, with long black hair.
4. A. Please give this to Mrs. Bacon on the fifth floor.
B. I'm sorry, but I'm new here. What does she look like?
A. She's tall, with blonde hair.
5. A. Please give this to Mr. Lopez on the second floor.
B. I'm sorry, but I'm new here. What does he look like?
A. He's short, with curly dark hair.
6. A. Please give this to Mr. Andersen in Shipping.
B. I'm sorry, but I'm new here. What does he look like?
A. He's short, with straight blond hair.
7. A. Please give this to Michael on the first floor.
B. I'm sorry, but I'm new here. What does he look like?
A. He's tall and thin.
8. A. Please give this to Ms. Dawson in Personnel.
B. I'm sorry, but I'm new here. What does she look like?
A. She's short, with curly dark hair.

Page 54

Listen and circle the word you hear.

1. A. Can you fix the TV?
B. Yes. I can fix it.
2. A. How often does your supervisor meet with you and your co-workers?
B. She meets with us every week.
3. A. Mr. Smith, you're training me very well.
B. Thank you, Brian.
4. A. Please give this to Mr. Gomez in Personnel.
B. Okay. I'll do it right away.
5. A. Can you help Jane stack the shelves?
B. Yes. I can help her right now.
6. A. Can you design office buildings?
B. Yes. I can design them very well.

7. A. I'm on vacation this week. Do you miss me?
   B. Of course we do. Everybody misses you!
8. A. Am I shampooing Mr. Davis all right?
   B. Yes. You're shampooing him very well.
9. A. Where do you want these beds?
   B. Put them in the bedroom.

Page 55

Listen and circle the word you hear.

1. A. What day is it?
   B. It's Monday.
2. A. Are you busy today?
   B. Yes. I'm going to visit my grandmother.
3. A. Are you busy after work?
   B. Yes. I coach my daughter's soccer team every Thursday.
4. A. What are you going to do after work today?
   B. I'm going to take a guitar lesson.
5. A. Are you busy after work today?
   B. What day is it?
   A. It's Wednesday.
   B. I'm afraid I'm busy today. I work out at the gym on Wednesday.
6. A. What day is it?
   B. Hmm. I think it's Wednesday. No. It's Friday.
   A. Thanks.

Page 58

Listen and decide if the following statements are true or false.

1. I often write to my parents.
2. I rarely see my sister.
3. I always talk to my parents on the weekend.
4. Sometimes I call my husband on my car phone.
5. I never lose touch with my friends.
6. I usually go out with my girlfriend on Saturday nights.
7. I rarely visit my grandmother. She lives far away.
8. I usually go downtown on the bus.
9. Bob and I don't see each other very often, but we always talk on the telephone.
10. I never use my fax machine.
11. If you have something important to tell Dr. Wu, you can always call him at his office, send him a fax, or beep him on his beeper.

Page 60

Listen and circle the correct answer.

1. A. What kind of TV shows do you like?
   B. I like sitcoms.
2. A. What kind of movies do you like?
   B. I like cartoons.

3. A. What kind of music do you like?
   B. I like rap music.
4. A. Tell me, what kind of music do you like?
   B. I like country music.
5. A. What's your favorite TV program?
   B. I like "Zootime."
6. A. What's your favorite TV program?
   B. I like "I Miss You." That's my favorite.

Page 64

Listen to the pharmacist's directions and choose the correct answer.

1. The cold medicine is on the top shelf.
2. The aspirin is on the middle shelf.
3. There are ear drops on the bottom shelf.
4. The throat lozenges are in Aisle 5.
5. We have cough syrup near the front of the shelf.
6. The medicine for stomachaches is in the back.
7. Maxi-Fed Cold Medicine is in the front near the cash register.
8. Brown's Pain Pills are on the bottom shelf.

Page 66

Listen and circle the correct time.

1. Can you come in this morning at 11:30?
2. How about today at 12:00?
3. Can you come in tomorrow at 3:15?
4. How about this afternoon at 4:45?
5. Can you come in today at 2:00?
6. How about Wednesday at 10:45?
7. Thursday at 8:15 in the morning?
8. Can you come in Monday evening at 6:45?
9. How about tomorrow at 9:30?

Page 70

Listen to the conversations and answer the questions.

Conversation 1

A. I'm concerned about your blood pressure, Mr. White.
B. My blood pressure?
A. Yes. You should change your diet.
B. I see.
A. I suggest you stop eating salty and fatty foods.
B. I understand.

Conversation 2

A. I'm concerned about your lungs, Mr. Martinez.
B. My lungs?
A. Yes. You should stop smoking. I suggest you quit immediately.
B. I understand. Thank you for the advice.

Page 73

Listen to the conversations and answer the questions.

Conversation 1

A. 911.
B. I want to report an emergency!
A. Yes?
B. My husband is choking and can't breathe!
A. What's your name?
B. Marjorie Miller. M-I-L-L-E-R.
A. And the address?
B. 15 Draper Avenue.
A. All right. An ambulance will be there right away.

Conversation 2

A. Police Emergency Unit.
B. I want to report an emergency!
A. Yes?
B. I think there's a burglar in my apartment!
A. What's your name?
B. Bill Richards.
A. And the address?
B. 324 Center Street.
A. Telephone number?
B. 367-9805.
A. All right. The police will be there right away.

Conversation 3

A. Fire Department.
B. I want to report an emergency!
A. Yes?
B. My house is on fire!
A. What's your name?
B. Emelia Sanchez.
A. And the address?
B. 40 Blake Street.
A. All right. The Fire Department will be there right away.

Page 75

Listen and write the number you hear.

1. Can you come in tomorrow morning at nine forty-five?
2. Take three capsules a day.
3. The address is thirty-four twenty-one Park Lane.
4. The medicine is in Aisle eleven.
5. The apartment has four bedrooms.
6. The rent is eight hundred and five dollars a month.

Page 76

Listen and circle the word you hear.

1. I'm looking for a dress.
2. Dresses are over there.
3. Where are the suits?
4. I suggest this sweater.
5. Hats are on that counter.
6. This pair of boots is very nice.
7. Are you looking for a raincoat?
8. I'm looking for pajamas.
9. What a nice evening gown!
10. Pants are on that rack.
11. Jackets are in the front of the store.

12. Are you looking for a jersey?

Page 80

Listen and choose the correct answer.

1. A. How does the blouse fit?
   B. This blouse is too small.
2. A. What's the problem?
   B. These pants are too short.
3. A. How does the suit fit?
   B. It's too tight.
4. A. What's the matter?
   B. This skirt is too big. I want to try on another one.
5. A. How do the socks fit?
   B. They're too large.
6. A. May I help you?
   B. Yes, please. These sneakers are too tight. I want to try on another pair.

Page 82

Listen and circle the amount of money you hear.

1. That's thirty-four fifty.
2. That comes to three hundred and five dollars and ninety-nine cents.
3. That's fourteen dollars, please.
4. That comes to four hundred and fifty-five dollars and fifty cents.
5. That's seventeen-fifty, please.
6. That comes to sixty-seven ninety-eight.
7. That's seventy dollars, please.
8. That comes to two hundred and forty-five dollars and fifty cents.
9. That's one hundred and two dollars and twenty cents.

Page 84

Listen and choose the correct answer.

Conversation 1

A. May I help you?
B. Yes. I want to return this shirt.
A. I see. What's the matter with it?
B. It's too tight.
A. Do you want to exchange it?
B. No. I'd like a refund, please.
A. Okay. Do you have the receipt?
B. Yes. Here you are.

Conversation 2

A. May I help you?
B. Yes. I want to return this bathrobe.
A. I see. What's the matter with it?
B. It's too heavy.
A. Do you want to exchange it?
B. No. I'd like a refund, please.
A. All right. Do you have the receipt?
B. I'm sorry. I don't.

Page 86

Listen to the conversation and answer the questions.

A. I'd like to mail these packages.
B. Where are they going?
A. To Hong Kong.
B. How do you want to send them?
A. Third class, please.
B. Do you want to insure them?
A. Hmm. I don't know.
B. Well, are they valuable?
A. Yes, they are. They're English textbooks and videogames. Please insure them for sixty dollars.
B. Okay. That comes to seven dollars and thirteen cents, please.

Page 87

Listen and circle the sentence you hear.

1. A. What are you going to do this weekend?
   B. I'm going to clean my garage.
2. A. What are your children going to do tonight?
   B. They're going to do their homework.
3. A. What's your husband going to do this Saturday?
   B. He's going to relax at home.
4. A. What's Mrs. Albert going to do today?
   B. She's going to visit her grandchildren.
5. A. What are you going to do this weekend?
   B. I'm going to visit my grandmother.
6. A. What are you and your classmates going to do this weekend?
   B. We're going to study English.
7. A. What's Martha going to do on Sunday?
   B. She's going to take her children to the zoo.

Page 91

Listen to the temperatures in Fahrenheit and Centigrade. Write the numbers you hear.

Good morning from the Weather Channel. Here is the weather report around the world. It's cloudy today in Beijing. The temperature there is 50°F/10°C. It's sunny today in Paris. The temperature there is 68°F/20°C. It's a hazy day in New York. The temperature there is 60°F/18°C. And it's hot today in Caracas. The temperature there is 95°F/35°C. It's hot and humid today in Manila. The temperature there is 93°F/34°C. It's raining in Chicago today. The temperature there is 50°F/10°C.

It's snowing in Anchorage. The temperature there is 32°F/0°C. And it's foggy today in San Francisco. The temperature there is 72°F/22°C. That's today's weather report around the world.

Page 95

Listen to the conversations and answer the questions.

Conversation 1

A. Let's do something outdoors today.
B. All right. But I don't want to go skiing. We went skiing last weekend.
A. Okay. What do you want to do?
B. I want to go skating.
A. All right. That sounds like fun.

Conversation 2

A. Let's do something outdoors today.
B. All right. But I don't want to go sailing. We went sailing yesterday.
A. Okay. What do you want to do?
B. I want to go swimming.
A. All right. That sounds like fun.

Page 98

Listen to the conversation and answer yes or no.

A. What do you like to do for exercise?
B. I like to play golf. How about you?
A. I like to go jogging.
B. Did you go jogging today?
A. Yes, I did. I went jogging after work. How about you? Did you play golf today?
B. Yes, I did. I played golf this morning.
A. Oh. That's nice.

Page 100

Listen and choose the correct response.

1. Where's the men's bathroom?
2. How do you want to send this package?
3. Excuse me. Can you help me?
4. What's she going to do tonight?
5. I'd like to buy this camera.
6. I'm looking for a belt.
7. What's the matter with those books?
8. What do you want to do this afternoon?
9. Did you have a good weekend?
10. What do you like to do for exercise?
11. Do you want to go to the beach tomorrow morning?
12. What did you do today?

CORRELATION
ExpressWays Student Text/Activity Workbook

Student Text Pages	Activity Workbook Pages
Exit 1	
2–3	1
4–5	2
6–7	3
8–9	4–5
10–11	6–7
12–15	8–11
Exit 2	
18–19	12
20–21	13–14
22–23	15–16
24–25	17
26–29	18–19
30–31	20–22
Exit 3	
34–39	23–25
40–41	26
42–43	27–28
44–45	29
46–47	30
48–49	31
50–51	32–33
Exit 4	
56–57	36
58–59	37–38
60–61	39–41
62–63	42–43
64–65	44
66–67	45
68–69	46
70–71	47

Student Text Pages	Activity Workbook Pages
Exit 5	
74–75	48
76–77	49–50
78–79	51
80–81	52
82–83	53–54
84–85	55–56
86–87	57–58
88–89	59–61
Exit 6	
92–93	62
94–95	63–64
96–97	65–66
98–99	67–68
100–101	69
102–103	70–71
104–105	72
106–107	73
Exit 7	
112–113	76–77
114–115	78–79
116–117	80
118–119	81
120–123	82–83
124–125	84
126–127	85
128–129	86
Exit 8	
132–133	87–88
134–137	89–91
138–139	92
140–143	93–94
144–145	95
146–149	96–97
150–151	98